# PRODUCTIVE SCHOOL SYSTEMS FOR A NONRATIONAL WORLD

Jerry L. Patterson, Stewart C. Purkey, and Jackson V. Parker

125 North West Street
Alexandria, VA 22314-2798
Association for Supervision and Curriculum Development

# Acknowledgments

We wish to acknowledge those who have influenced our thoughts and writing of this manuscript. In particular, we appreciate the critique of earlier drafts by J. Howard Johnston, Mary Metz, and Fred Newmann, as well as the ASCD reviewers.

Ronald S. Brandt, Executive Editor
Nancy Carter Modrak, Manager of Publications
Jo Ann Irick Jones, Managing Editor
Janet Frymoyer, Production Coordinator
Al Way, Art Director

ASCD publications present a variety of viewpoints. The views expressed or implied in this book are not necessarily official positions of the Association.

Price: $7.50
ASCD Stock Number: 611-86022
ISBN: 0-87120-136-4
Library of Congress Card Catalog Number: 86-71233

# Contents

10/27/86 Pub. 5.0.

# Foreword

Few treatises, tales, or texts fulfill expectations; this one far exceeds them. Be prepared for an instructive and constructive examination of that elusive structure called "the organization." Although readers will not be disappointed, they are quite likely to discern, doubt, and perhaps discard many assumptions held near and dear for a long time.

The authors embark on a seemingly impossible quest to view order in chaos, if not to bring order to it. They deserve high commendation for their noble cause, higher for their conscientious effort, and still higher for their obvious success.

Their cause is simple: to restore efficacy—the ability to make a positive difference in children's education—to the teachers in America' schools. To do so, say the authors, requires viewing and understanding organizations in general, school districts and schools in particular, as nonrational.

Readers are urged to be undeterred by the enormous challenge laid before them in the descriptions of the forces of change. Demographic shifts, federal and state demands, collective bargaining, and teacher supply are sufficient to overwhelm. But those who accept these as prelude and continue reading will be rewarded.

The bureaucratic model, or rational system, is compared and contrasted with an emerging view of reality identified as nonrational. Imaginary but convincing vignettes of typical school situations boldly highlight differences regarding organizational goals, power, decision making, external environment, and teaching process.

The authors do more than advocate the nonrational model as more responsive to the only certainty—change. They provide three strategies that can create integrated organizational structures: managing the organizational culture, strategic planning, and empowerment. Each is a fascinating concept in its own right. Collectively they reinforce the potential of the nonrational model to the school district.

The authors also devote some attention to the concept of leadership in converting vision into organizational reality. Successful leaders are expected to create a flow of purposeful and unifying images throughout the organizational culture; to combine skills of historian and futurist in scanning, monitoring, and interpreting the environment and the organization in strategic planning; and to enable people and units to access support, information, and resources through empowerment.

Although their principal focus is on district-level organization, the authors devote ample attention to applying the nonrational model at the building level.

The authors draw upon sociology, corporate studies, and effective schools research to make their case. And they make it exceedingly well. In such an involved construct, some meandering or loss of focus might be expected and accepted. Such is not the situation. The story is crisp, clear, and concise. It starts well, builds at an appropriate rate, and comes together in the final pages.

The book has a significant lesson. For those who learn it, the restoration of efficacy to schools in a nonrational world becomes not only possible, but probable.

—GERALD R. FIRTH
*ASCD President, 1986–87*

# Introduction

## CHANGE: THE ONLY CERTAINTY

In 1980, a newly appointed superintendent of schools called the administrative staff together and, as part of the introductory message, announced: "You have been through some tough times lately—including a lengthy teacher strike and serious budget strife. But I can tell you with some certainty that we are entering a period of stability. We've survived the crisis periods, and you can expect very little change or disruption from the district's long-range plan."

Today the administrative staff is still looking for signs of stability. Realistically, though, most of us in the education business have finally concluded that change is the most stable thing on which we can depend.

Acknowledging that we are educating in an era of change and uncertainty is not enough. We need to understand the major causes for these unstable conditions and the consequences for educational practice.

We do know we are charged with educating a more complex and diverse student population than ever before. Moreover, changes in the entire demographic character of the United States have drastically altered the social structure. Consequently, our children have to be prepared for a world even more uncertain than the world of today.

But a changing population is only one force creating instability. Federal and state governments have lobbied for and legislated changes in a dramatic and far-reaching effort to raise standards while providing equal access for all. At the same time, the various constituencies that make up "the community" for any educational system have expanded their demands and expectations. Often, these expectations are contradictory, as in the demands for increased services and simultaneous cost reductions. More often, the contradictions are subtle and ambiguous, dealing with shades of meaning, differing values, or questions of emphasis. Sometimes the demands conflict with the legislated mandates—either inadvertently, or on purpose.

## THE CONSEQUENCES: A LOSS OF EFFICACY

This complex web of uncertainty, conflict, and contradiction has reduced public confidence in the effectiveness of our school organizations and the people who work in them. Similarly, many educators feel a loss of efficacy—the power to make a difference in children's education. Teachers feel a loss of the power to make a difference when faced by children with more diverse needs and by communities that seem only to criticize where once they praised. Administrators wonder aloud what happened to the good old days when things were still under control. Such conflicting demands and expectations force a retreat to traditional methods and "safe" practices that, ironically, don't work. There is even divisiveness within the ranks. Pitted against the administration by a rocky history of collective bargaining, which has won some measurable gains at some unmeasurable but significant costs, teachers perceive little help forthcoming from their supposed leaders. Administrators see their position and effectiveness eroded by the same history of events.

## THE CORRECTIVE ACTION: PRODUCTIVE SCHOOL SYSTEMS FOR A NONRATIONAL WORLD

Fortunately, things aren't as bleak as they appear on the surface. First, the recent research on effective schools points to clear direction for restoring efficacy in an era of change. In addition to the literature on effective schools, two other lines of inquiry are helpful in guiding educators. The field of sociology issues a challenge to the belief that organizations are rational systems. Instead, organizations are more realistically described as nonrational.[1] This change in model for thinking about organizations carries with it significant implications for how school districts should approach organizational structure, planning, decision making, and leadership. Similar conclusions have been reached in a different field. The corporate reform literature on excellence contains some key findings from successful corporations, which offer important direction for school districts.

*Productive School Systems for a Nonrational World* draws upon the areas of sociology, corporate studies, and effective schools research to develop a solid foundation for understanding how educational organizations operate in a nonrational world. Building on this foundation, we provide concrete examples of how this organizational theory translates into effective practices for

---

[1] Use of the term "nonrational" does not mean that organizations don't make sense. It means that they don't follow the ideal, orderly logic that rational organizational theory assumes. Instead, they follow a complex logic that at times seems paradoxical or contradictory, but that is nevertheless understandable and controllable. Chapters 3 and 4 expand on the meaning of this concept.

creating productive and innovative organizations, for implementing new strategies of planning and decision making to make use of this new organization, and for developing the kind of leadership that assures the organization will produce a renewed sense of efficacy. While our primary focus is on district-level organization, we also give substantial attention to applying the model at the school level.

Clearly, some schools can go it alone. Our firm conviction, however, is that the power to make a sustained difference in schooling can be best achieved through the framework developed in this book.

# Educating in an
# Era of Change

_____

_____

_____

_____

_____

## INTRODUCTION

In this era of uncertainty, a few things are known for sure. Demands on our schools and teachers have increased and changed in ways no one expected.

• Children are entering our schoolhouse doors as a more diverse group with more complex needs than ever before.

• Demands emanating from state and federal levels exert increasing pressures on schools to change.

• Community expectations for schools have multiplied over the last several years, and often these expectations conflict with the traditional missions of education, with state and federal demands, and/or with themselves.

• Collective bargaining has had a major impact on all aspects of education.

• The schools find themselves in a constant state of fiscal uncertainty.

• Retirements, defections from the teaching ranks, and an increasing student enrollment are leading to a national teacher shortage.

Consequently, the educator's sense of efficacy, the power to make a positive difference in children's lives, is shrinking in the face of these forces of change.

This chapter describes these forces at work. Since the foremost change deals with the clients of education themselves, the children, we explore these forces in greater depth. Although we treat the remaining forces somewhat more briefly, we will show the emerging complexity when these changes interact with the changing clientele.

We look first at who the students are.[1] The picture can be unsettling.

# THE FORCES OF CHANGE

## Demographic Changes

Children are entering our schools from more distressed circumstances than any time in history. This picture contradicts our rational view of America as a country where virtually all children have enough food, clothing, shelter, education, health care, and family support. Instead, we see an America where demographic changes in many areas, including family structure, income, age structure, ethnic makeup, and adolescent stress converge to describe a student population very different from school children of the past.

*More students from diverse backgrounds.* The United States is experiencing a marked shift in racial composition, particularly in the school-age population. Currently, 25 percent of that population is from minority backgrounds. However, in all but two of the 25 largest school systems, seven out of ten students are minorities. In addition, our country is educating and socializing the greatest wave of immigrants since 1902, about 14 million people. Most come from non-Western cultures and language groups; while 15 percent are illiterate in their own language, others are so brilliant as to shake our confidence in our own backgrounds.

*More children from nontraditional families.* The typical American family of the 1950s—consisting of the father at work, the mother at home, and two children at school—is the mythical family of the 1980s, representing less than 10 percent of all families. Increased divorce rates contribute to much of the change in family structure. So do the remarriages of divorced people, creating instant new family arrangements, few of which are well understood and most of which affect children. Given current trends, approximately half of the children living in the United States today will spend some part of their life

---

[1] This section draws on a variety of demographic sources. For a summary, see Feistritzer (1985a) and Hodgkinson (1985).

prior to age 18 living with one biological parent. The need for such a term as "biological parent" is itself an indicator of powerful change at work.

*More poor children.* In 1982, the official Census Bureau measure of poverty rose to the highest rate since 1963: 11 percent for whites, 26 percent for Hispanics, and 34 percent for blacks. In particular, children are disproportionately poor. Since 1979, the number of children living below the poverty line has increased to the point that about 25 percent of all children under the age of 18 are living in poverty—one out of two black children, two out of five Hispanics, and one out of seven white children.

*More adolescent stress.* Several different indicators point to the fact that adolescents are experiencing more stress in their lives than ever before. The abuse statistics show that in 1983, 1.5 million cases were reported, an increase of 200,000 from 1982. Nationally, suicide is the second largest killer of persons 15–24 years of age.

Sexual activity among adolescents has increased by about two thirds in the last ten years. According to a recent study, the United States leads virtually all developed countries in rates of teenage sexual activity, births, and abortions.

*More children with handicapping conditions.* Since adoption of P.L. 94–142, we have mainstreamed over 600,000 students. With the exception of profoundly handicapped children, these young people now receive their education in the least restrictive environment possible. Teachers feel caught between the praiseworthy intent of this legislation and the real difficulties of implementing it, especially when they have no formal training in how to do it.

These demographic changes profoundly affect the educator's sense of efficacy. As more children come to our schools hungry, deprived in other ways, and from poorly understood social and cultural conditions, teachers find that they must attend to some very basic needs before quality learning can occur. Without formal training in appropriate teaching techniques and minimal adaptations in curriculums, teachers report a growing sense of inadequacy in reaching many of these students. For example, teachers confirm that academic learning time competes with time students need for coping with more basic matters that have little to do with schooling.

Even though these demographic changes have had the most telling impact on changes occurring in our schools, educators are quick in pointing to other significant forces at work.

## Federal and State Demands

Spurred by the various national reports, federal and state legislatures have ridden into the fray to save schools with the dual goals of raising standards and being reelected. Legislation has variously increased graduation requirements, required minimum competency testing for teachers and students, defined what textbooks should contain, authorized longer school days and years, supported early childhood education and birth control for teens, and advocated merit pay and career ladders for teachers. Never has so vast and specific an educational agenda been set by noneducators (Kirst 1984). Consideration of the impact of such reforms by the legislators has generally been simplistic. Most of the reforms, and the reports they are based on, can be distilled into three themes: higher standards, common leaner curriculums, and fewer student options. According to Raywid, Tesconi, and Warren (1984), these themes are impoverished in at least six ways. The reports and legislative actions:

1. provide little convincing evidence for their major claim that schools are failing;

2. judge schools on only one of their many missions—the academic one;

3. provide no logic for the effects that might come from the proposals;

4. pay slight attention to the forces that link school success to class, race, ethnicity, and gender;

5. isolate schools from their external policy environment, most notably in not identifying funding for the reforms; and

6. present little attention to educational purpose; they demonstrate no vision.

Clearly teachers feel that they have been consulted about none of the proposed reforms such as career ladders, merit pay, and competency testing, even though much of it was done in the name of improving the profession. But its impact is already being felt on their lives.

## Growth in Community Expectations

There was a time when the purposes of schooling were virtually unchallenged. But today, various constituencies within the community expect the role of the school to be expanded in regard to their particular issue. At the same time, other constituencies claim that the schools have taken on too much. Schools are expected to teach English as a second language and provide instruction on sex, health, computers, drugs, peace, nuclear issues, and driving cars. Schools should do all this while building character, returning to the basics, desegregating society, plus ensuring excellence and equity.

And, we should do it all for less money. This view is held by many citizens who, because they have no children in the schools, apparently feel that they have no direct stake in the quality of education. Americans over 65 outnumber today's teenagers. They are a powerful interest group, voting more than any age group while drawing support from all younger adults advocating for their parents' and their own retirements. Over 70 percent of our country's families have no children in school. It will take very persuasive tactics to convince these people that education is a citizen responsibility, not just a parental responsibility, in order that a healthy society be maintained.

## The Constant Fiscal Crisis

Taxpayers have effectively revolted against the property tax in efforts like Proposition 13 (California) and Proposition 2½ (Massachusetts), gutting public education of its resources. Failed levies and bond referenda are routine. Cost is usually the first consideration in any new proposal. Educators frantically juggle the books and reallocate resources in order to meet the expanding demands while trying to conduct reduction in force programs with as little disruption of service as possible. People say close schools and save money—until it's their school, when they turn around and fight the proposed cost savings. Revenue shortfalls, changes in land values, and industry requests for tax give-backs so they can survive not only affect the schools, but do so willy-nilly, in ways hard to foresee. A recent Gallup Poll (Gallup 1985) indicated a majority of the national sample (52 percent) would vote against raising taxes for the schools, even if the local schools said there was a need. Even parents with children in the public schools failed to turn out a majority, with only 46 percent willing to vote for such an increase.

## The Impact of Collective Bargaining

Another significant force affecting education has been the rise of collective bargaining. Johnson (1984, p. 5) has remarked, "Collective bargaining has, various authors conclude, increased the formal authority of teachers and restricted the formal authority of principals, centralized and standardized school practices, redefined and reduced teachers' work obligation, and increased teachers' job protection." Even those who would moderate this claim find it difficult to deny that collective bargaining has, indeed, contributed to the changing conditions in education. It has formalized in many ways the relationships between and among school people, parents, and children.

## Decline in Quality and Quantity of Teachers

Projections from the National Center for Education Statistics indicate we will need to hire 1.65 million additional teachers in the next eight years to meet demand (Feistritzer 1985b, p. 8). According to Linda Darling-Hammond

(1984), this situation is partly caused by disgruntled teachers leaving the profession and compounded by the fact that teachers who are most dissatisfied with the profession are those with the best academic preparation. Based on current data, teacher vacancies will be filled by college graduates who score among the lowest on national tests and who have lower grade point averages than their classmates entering more "lucrative" careers.

Many important questions are raised as teacher preparation institutions, state certification departments, unions, and local school districts struggle with this projected shortage. Teacher preparation institutions, smarting from criticism of their current programs, are looking to upgrade the quality without discouraging prospective students. State departments would like to make certification tougher. Unions would like to keep the supply side down so the demand side, and the price of teachers, could go up. School districts know they will need a lot of new teachers soon, and would prefer that numbers and quality would be up, but price down.

## A DECLINING SENSE OF EFFICACY

Earlier we defined efficacy as the ability to make a positive difference in students' lives. Particularly in the face of the powerful forces we have just outlined, it is not surprising that educators' sense of efficacy is declining. As Darling-Hammond (1984) points out, even the altruistic reward of seeing young people grow has declined as the nature of teaching has changed.

## A FOUNDATION FOR RESTORING EFFICACY: PRODUCTIVE SCHOOL SYSTEMS FOR A NONRATIONAL WORLD

One could conclude from our remarks that there is no hope. Nothing could be further from the truth; there is light at the end of the tunnel and it is not the headlight of an onrushing locomotive. Educators' sense of effectiveness and importance can be restored.

First, however, a new foundation must be built for understanding our organizations. This will require personal effort on the part of educators and lay leaders in understanding a new way of thinking about the world of school organizations. But, once that effort is undertaken, a foundation can be built for effective action.

We believe this foundation, and the framework built on it, represents a step forward in the maturation of our knowledge about how educational organizations work. Because the forces outlined in this chapter have created much of the instability we all sense but have trouble articulating, we are compelled to step back and rethink how our world in general, and school districts in particular, operate within a framework of rapid change.

Throughout this book, we will argue that these forces of change can be understood and successfully managed; that a sense of efficacy is yet possible. We educators can regain that sense, if we are willing to try a different way of thinking about our world and our organizations.

Because this different way of thinking challenges current assumptions, it may be difficult initially for some people to accept. But our approach will have three main virtues for practitioners: first, it will "feel right" in its descriptions of the world in which schools operate; second, it has been demonstrated to work in the challenging world of private enterprise; and third, it will provide specific directions and a unified method for understanding and working in the existing world of school organizations. While our major emphasis will be on the restoration of organizational efficacy, the strategies presented for making organizations effective are designed ultimately to empower those within the organization to make a positive difference with children.

## ASSUMPTIONS: OLD AND NEW

The world is characterized by change, and schools are struggling to respond. We suggest that the prevailing way of thinking about school organizations comes from five entrenched assumptions about the world in which educators work. Somehow these assumptions have escaped close examination, even in light of the changing conditions we have discussed. Throughout this book we will consistently challenge these old, entrenched assumptions and demonstrate that a new set of assumptions more accurately describes the world in which we as educators work. For now, we offer a taste of what's to come. Below we summarize the contrast between the old and the new along five dimensions.

1. Organizational Goals
   - *Old Assumption:* School systems are guided by a single set of uniform goals.
   - *New Assumption:* School systems are necessarily guided by multiple and sometimes competing sets of goals.

2. Power
   - *Old Assumption:* Power in school systems is (and should be) located at the top.
   - *New Assumption:* Power in school systems is distributed throughout the organization.

3. Decision Making
   - *Old Assumption:* Decision making in school systems is a logical problem-solving process that arrives at the one best solution.
   - *New Assumption:* Decision making in school systems in inevitably a bargaining process to arrive at solutions that satisfy a number of constituencies.

4. External Environment
   - *Old Assumption:* The public is supportive of school systems and influences them in predictable and marginal ways.
   - *New Assumption:* The public legitimately influences school systems in major ways that are sometimes unpredictable.

5. Teaching Process
   - *Old Assumption:* There is one best way to teach for maximum educational effectiveness.
   - *New Assumption:* There are a variety of situationally appropriate ways to teach that are optimally effective.

# FROM ASSUMPTIONS TO PRACTICALITY

Where do all of these assumptions lead us? To begin with, let's see where the old assumptions have taken us. The traditional school organizational assumptions outlined above underlie what is called the *rational* model of organizations. This rational model leads to a segmented organizational structure. According to Kanter (1983), segmentalism is concerned with compartmentalizing things and keeping them isolated from one another. Such an organizational approach defines problems in a narrow perspective, independent of their context within the larger organization. We concur with Kanter that the segmented organizational structure founded on the old assumptions is inelastic and incapable of adapting to the changing realities facing contemporary organizations.

In contrast, the new assumptions lead to a new perspective we call the nonrational model of organizations. This model, in turn, leads to an integrated approach to organizational structure. As conceptualized by Kanter (1983), integrated thinking moves beyond received wisdom to combine ideas from multiple perspectives into meaningful wholes. Issues are seen in context of the total organization. This nonrational model, with its integrated organizational structure, is responsive to the changes we have described in this chapter. And, as we will demonstrate in the chapters to come, adoption of this view leads immediately to three strategies that can create those integrated structures. These strategies are *managing the organizational culture, strategic planning, and empowerment.* Each is the subject of a chapter. Finally, we develop the concept of leadership in the context of the nonrational model for organizations, including the skills by which a leader implements the strategies leading to integrated structures.

Throughout this book, we will build a strong case that the nonrational model is our best bet for creating school systems that work most effectively. At this point, educators may raise two objections as we begin to build our case. First, they may object that we are discussing matters far removed from the front lines of teaching and learning. Second, they may protest that our borrowing from the private sector literature on organizations is inappropriate. They will point to a basic difference: education has no firm and clear "bottom line" to measure success like the profit margin does in business and industry. They will assert that this difference is fundamental, and little transfer between the two worlds is possible.

We both agree and disagree with the first objection. In this book, we are creating a framework for thinking about school organizations. We are not talking about the quality of instruction in schools, as important as that is, but about changing the behavior of organizations. It should be clear that organizational behavior can affect the quality of instruction. Neither are we talking about improving curricular content, but we are talking about ways to make wise decisions about such content. Obviously, then, discussions about organizational variables can be relevant to teaching and learning.

We reject the second objection. We admit that we will not say much about educational bottom lines other than some very general remarks. Rather, our discussion focuses on organizational criteria that, when realized, can achieve output criteria set by individual districts. These organizational criteria include the ideas that a good organization is flexible, uses integrated structures, monitors its organizational culture, develops strategic planning techniques, and empowers its people. However, each district will have to set its own output criteria and gather appropriate data to assess the degree of successful achievement.

We argue that the nonrational model will improve teaching and learning, which, after all, is the bottom line of education. Within this mission, organizations will have a variety of short-, medium-, and long-term goals that may conflict internally as well as with those of other districts. Disagreements can set in as educators get more specific. Leaders have some obligations to bring order to goals that go astray in this world. But they must not do this in a simpleminded way. We will argue that the nonrational approach provides the most effective way to bring creative and effective order to the complexities of conflicting and competing goals.

Before developing this model, it is appropriate to discuss in more detail the assumptions and concepts of the rational model that has shaped school districts and given education much of its present character.

# 2

# The Prevailing Condition: Educational Organizations as Rational Systems

_____

_____

_____

_____

_____

## INTRODUCTION

For most of this century, the rational model has been the dominant framework for explaining and analyzing how organizations work. The study of educational organizations shows no departure from this trend. Traditionally, the actions of educational policymakers have been based on the assumption that educational organizations are rational systems (Callahan 1962). In general, "rational" implies reasonable, sensible, and having exercised sound judgment. Applied to organizations, to behave rationally is to behave logically, making clear connections between goals, organizational structures, activities, and outcomes. Although many educators will argue that this is the way school districts *should* function, the major intent of this chapter is not to argue for the rational model as a basis for describing what *ought to be* but rather to describe a deeply rooted conception of how school districts, as organizations, *do* function. It represents one view of reality as documented by organizational theory and organizational practice. Specifically, in the next section, we illustrate this image of reality through a brief hypothetical case study of the Omega School District applying the rational model to a key set of decisions. In the final section, we amplify the meaning of rationality by examining the rational model along five dimensions of educational organizations: (1) organizational goals, (2) power, (3) decision making, (4) external environment, and (5) teaching process. Before diving into an analysis of these concepts, let's focus on a rational school district in action.

## THE OMEGA SCHOOL DISTRICT STUDY

In September 1980, Omega Superintendent of Schools Barbara Howell called the senior administrative team together for an important meeting. A condensed version of the meeting is described below. Superintendent Howell began the meeting by reviewing for new team members the policymaking process in Omega District.

For those of you new to the team, it may be helpful to outline how policy is determined in our district. Of course, ultimately policy decisions are made by the board of education. Historically, though, the senior administrative team identifies the most important goals the district should address in the next three-year cycle. This is accomplished through a very calculated process involving this team's perceptions of the needs of the organization. To put it bluntly, if we are going to be held responsible for leadership in this district, we should be in a position to determine the direction of the district. Once direction is set, it also becomes our responsibility to see that the goals are clearly transmitted to all levels of the district, culminating in a set of instructional objectives that are taught in the classroom. Now I know that places a heavy burden on all of us in the room, but there is no way to duck it. We are ultimately accountable to the public for what goes on in those classrooms.

Once we set our instructional goals, we have a carefully defined training process for teachers in preparing them to implement goals. Next, we always evaluate our goals by linking performance of students to the goals of the organization. This is the true test of our efficiency in delivering on our promises.

Admittedly, sometimes we miss the mark because we aren't aware of information that would have affected our decision. When this happens, we reconvene this team and, with the added or new information, make necessary adjustments in policy and goals, which get translated into revised practices in the classroom.

This is the approach to decision making we have always followed in this organization. I believe it is the rational way to run an organization. And, so the literature tells us, it is the hallmark of successful organizations.

With this bit of history for background, let me relate it to our present issue.

As you well know, the topic of computers continues to be an important issue. Although very few school districts at this point have ventured into this arena in a serious way, I am convinced that Omega District needs to determine the most efficient use of computers in our district and proceed to develop a three-year implementation plan. I have discussed this issue with each of you independently, and I feel there is unanimous support to go full speed ahead.

Therefore, I have asked Assistant Superintendent Leonard Hansen to form a task force of the instructional coordinators, make a determination of the most efficient use of computers in Omega District, and report recommendations to this administrative team within six months. At that time we will present a three-year plan to the board.

In the meantime, it would not be efficient to purchase any more computers without clear direction based on the district's goals for computers. Since we have a few scattered computers in the district, I'm asking Dr. Hansen to please direct the principals affected to hold back on using their units until the district can come to grips with a long-range plan.

Any questions?

After several clarifying questions were asked and answered, Assistant Superintendent Hansen set about the task of briefing the committee of instructional coordinators on the nature of the issue, then developing a plan of action as described below.

Hansen's committee agreed that the first step was to review the literature on computers and determine the available options for consideration by the district. After three weeks of intensive study, a volunteer who researched the literature reported that computer use could be broken down into four major categories:

- computer-assisted learning,
- computer-managed instruction,
- computer literacy, and
- administrative applications.

In deciding which of these uses to be given first priority in the Omega School District, the computer committee felt the most logical approach would be to apply a common set of criteria to each computer application. By asking the same questions each time, the committee could compare the various uses of computers and arrive at a solid recommendation to the senior administrative team.

After much discussion, the committee agreed to apply the following criteria to each possible use:

- What is the educational justification for this use?
- Where can this be used most efficiently?
- What are the costs associated with this use?
- Is this use cost effective?

A lot of hard work yielded a determination of which computer applications were cost effective. Next, the committee needed to decide which computer uses have the highest priority. They applied four steps, outlined below, to arrive at their decision:

- Rank order the cost-effective applications according to need.

- Calculate how much equipment is required to serve the students.
- Calculate the estimated price associated with decisions in step two.
- Compare cost estimates to budget estimates and adjust where necessary.

After agonizing through this process, the committee concluded that computer literacy should be the priority for the Omega School District, and that a second-level use, computer-assisted learning, should not be a district goal until the first priority was achieved throughout the system.

The next step in the process was to develop a set of instructional objectives and accompanying teaching methods to best achieve the organization goal of computer literacy. After reviewing many curriculum guides, the committee settled on a computer literacy package developed by the San Amigo, California, School District. This package contained instructional objectives for each grade level, K–12, as well as teaching strategies to reach those objectives. Also included were test instruments correlated with the objectives so that the district could easily demonstrate its ability to achieve the organizational goal of computer literacy.

Plan in hand, the computer committee presented its recommendations right on schedule to the senior administrative team. Superintendent Howell led the team through a structured workshop to review the committee recommandations. After modifying some of the recommendations, the senior administrative team voted unanimously to forward the plan to the board of education.

About seven months from the initial meeting with the team, Superintendent Howell scheduled a meeting of the board of education. Howell began the meeting:

> Members of the board, I have called this meeting tonight to provide you with a set of recommendations in the area of computers. Before I get to the recommendations I want to review for you the steps the administrative team took to arrive at our recommendations.

Howell proceeded to describe the very rational process used by the senior administrative team and the instructional coordinator committee. She talked about the need to set organizational goals, identify the most important issues, gather all available information, consider all possible options within reach of the committee, and arrive at what they considered to be the best decision through professional judgment that maximized the attainment of organizational goals.

Howell concluded that she felt the recommendations were sound precisely because of the rational, problem-solving approach that had been followed, and she urged approval by the board.

After a brief discussion, the board unanimously approved the superintendent's recommendations, pending a public hearing on the topic.

The next week a hearing was conducted, and 30 community members registered to speak. All but one speaker gave unqualified endorsement to the plan and commended the superintendent for such a thorough process to arrive at the recommendations. They complimented the wealth of expertise in the district and felt that the district should have the right to implement any decision that was based on the best professional judgment of the organization. The lone dissenter argued that computer-assisted learning was the wave of the future and should be the number one priority of the district.

At the next board meeting, individual board members commented that the community had responded in a manner that was predictable, reflecting a rather stable pattern of community support over the last several years. Then the board formally voted to support a policy directing the Omega School District to develop and implement a three-year plan for teaching specified computer literacy objectives in all grades, and subsequently to measure the effectiveness of this goal through tests designed to match the objectives. Based on the evaluation results in three years, the board would decide whether to continue, modify, or drop the computer literacy goal.

Admittedly, the Omega School District study is fictitious. It is also exaggerated to dramatize the rational model in its purest sense, but nevertheless it describes an ideal that many school districts persistently try to implement. Consistent with our definition of rationality, people in the Omega District behaved in a logical fashion, designing a decision-making process that maintained a direct relationship between goals, activities, and expected outcomes. To the policymakers of the district, this logical course of action was the correct course of action because it fit with their rational view of reality.

However, in order to have a more comprehensive understanding of the rational model, we need to move beyond terms like logical and reasonable. The next section draws on the Omega example as we examine in more detail the meaning of rational systems.

## RATIONAL SYSTEMS

As sociologists study organizations, they carve them up in various ways to look at the respective parts.[1] No typology has been acknowledged to be the one best way to describe and understand organizations, but five distinct

---

[1] For an overview of typologies of organizations, see W. R. Scott, *Organizations: Rational, Natural and Open Systems* (Englewood Cliffs, N.J.: Prentice-Hall, 1981), chapter 2.

categories are recurrent in the literature: (1) organizational goals, (2) power, (3) decision making, (4) external environment, and (5) technology (or, in education, teaching process). We will apply this framework to our study of the rational model.

## Organizational Goals

Indelibly printed on the calling card of every rational organization is the motto, "We are goal oriented." To believe otherwise is to disavow the trademark of the rational model. This goal orientation permeates both the values and actions of school districts. They follow the logical process of setting goals, designing the most efficient strategies to implement these goals, and evaluating whether the goals have been accomplished. Even district policies are designed to improve the operation of the goal-oriented process; these policies tend to emphasize outcomes, accountability, and efficiency.

Since the organization's goals set the tone and direction for how the school district operates, they must be clearly stated and thoroughly understood by members of the organization. In general, the rational system cannot tolerate unclear and misunderstood organizational goals. Muddled or confused goals can lead to inefficient operating procedures and misdirected resources. To do this flies in the face of the meaning of rationality. Superintendent Howell of the Omega School District took a strong stand, arguing that before the district committed resources and energy, clearly defined direction for the use of computer technology was needed.

In rational systems, it is assumed that goals remain stable over time. This characteristic is critical to the long-term efficiency of the organization. As school districts invest scarce resources in efforts to achieve their goals, they cannot afford to be changing their goals constantly and thus changing their operating procedures. It becomes an expensive way to do business and hard to justify in the eyes of the taxpayer. Besides, stable goals create a sense of confidence within the district and to the public that the district knows with certainty what children will need well into the future.

To chart district direction, goals in a rational system are set by the leaders of the district. Since senior school district administrators and the board of education are ultimately held accountable for the success of the district, logically they should have a heavy hand in determining its direction. Through the investment of time and energy in arriving at goals, the leaders understandably develop a strong commitment to assuring that these goals are implemented.

In fact, to assure that organizational goals are realized, leaders within rational systems take the necessary steps to see that the goals are translated into specific objectives within subunits of the organization. In the case of instructional goals, the top-down transmission ideally results in lesson plans that are correlated with the overall educational goals of the district.

Within the Omega School District, the selection of computer literacy as a goal set in motion a series of training sessions for teachers designed to help them understand the district's definition of computer literacy and to train them to implement the new curriculum. In this way, the senior administrative team felt confident that the goal of computer literacy would be reached.

In summary, organizational goals within a rational system reflect a view of reality that says: (1) organizations are goal oriented; (2) these goals are clearly stated and understood by members of the organization; (3) once stated, the goals remain stable over time; (4) to chart district direction, district goals need to be determined by the leaders of the district; and (5) organizational goals gain strength by being translated into precise objectives within the district's subunits, taking final root in the lesson plans of classroom teachers.

## Power

"Power" is a loaded term. Depending on the audience, it can connote negative, as well as positive, messages. The word also has multiple nuances such as reward power, expert power, coercive power, and legitimate power (Kanter 1977). In studies of power, these fine gradations may be important. For our purposes, a more general definition serves equally well. Within the context of this discussion, power is the ability to mobilize energy within an organization to achieve identified goals. In short, it is the ability to "do," and thus it means having access to whatever is needed for the doing (Kanter 1977).

In rational systems, the formal organizational structure is the basis for power. The organizational chart provides clear evidence of the power relationships among those having various positions in the system. Organizational members understand that to have influence in the system, they need to follow tha bureaucratic chain of command. To violate this procedure is to violate one of the deeply rooted norms of rational systems.

Also, in rational systems, power comes in fixed quantities; there is a limit on the total "units" of empowerment available to the organization. For one person to gain power, someone else has to give up a comparable amount. This sort of scarce, finite resource becomes viewed as a precious commodity. Those holding the most power units hold the bulk of control over the organization's energy and direction.

Most power structures in rational organizations have the familiar pyramidal look. The real power to make things happen draws heavily from the top of the pyramid. The board of education and the superintendent wield the most influence. They have the vested authority to make the most important decisions. That is, they are empowered to set and carry out the organization's goals. Since power units are scarce and finite, power begets power. Administrators who are already acknowledged to have power through the organizational design can be more influential in getting people to do their bidding. By being able to mobilize resources due to their position in the organization, they reinforce the fact within the organization that the top segment of the pyramid has the most units of power to get things done.

In order that organizational goals may be carried out effectively, the rational model demands tightly coupled connections in the organizational structure. For example, if the superintendent expects the district goal of computer literacy to be realized, he or she needs to know with confidence that these expectations are clearly conveyed to the principals, who, in turn, clearly and precisely translate these expectations to the classroom teachers. Without such tight coupling in place among the many levels of the district, centralized power loses its grip on assuring the efficient implementation of organizational goals, particularly at the classroom level.

In rational systems, success is achieving organizational goals. As people within the organization demonstrate their ability to deliver results, the power brokers empower those rising stars through promotion to demonstrate further their ability to create success. Of course, accompanying added power through promotion is added accountability. Within the rational model, accountability is defined as the responsibility for demonstrating that outcomes have been met and that they fulfill the expectations designated by the organizational hierarchy. So a spiral effect is set in motion. With demonstrated success, individuals are promoted; promotion carries with it more accountability, which is associated with more leverage to mobilize resources. Since the mobilization of resources to get things done is the crux of power, moving up the organizational structure supplies greater doses of power to achieve organizational goals.

For example, the senior administrative team of the Omega School District was the recognized power bloc. They determined organizational goals. They controlled the available resources to see that the district's goals were achieved. With their collective wealth within the district's scarce supply of power, they even sought to govern how teachers should approach teaching the computer literacy curriculum. By empowering those at the top of the organizational structure, the district assumed that important decisions throughout the organization were carefully correlated with the official goals of the organization.

## Decision Making

Like the other dimensions within the rational model, the decision-making process follows an efficient, orderly pattern. Since the organization is goal oriented, decisions can't be made in the absence of goals to provide direction. The goals are determined through a logical, problem-solving process. In addition, as mentioned earlier, organizational goals are clearly stated, understood by the members of the organization, and remain stable over time. Not surprisingly, the leaders in rational systems rely heavily on the organizational goals to guide organizational decision making.

Decision making in rational systems focuses attention on those issues considered most important to the overall, long-term operation of the district. An efficiently operating school district can't justify the expenditure of resources on inconsequential issues, while major issues scream for action. The rational model not only assumes, but goes to great lengths to verify that a rational process is in place to determine which issues are the most significant to the goals and efficient functioning of the school district.

Once an issue has been identified, the district mobilizes resources to gather all the available information on the topic. Lack of information could result in making a poor decision, and the rational system has little tolerance for sloppy work. With information in hand, the decision makers consider all possible options, weighing carefully the relative merits of each option as it relates to organizational goals.

After all the data are in and analyzed in a very systematic way, the decision makers arrive at a one best solution, which maximizes the desirable outcomes for the organization. Realizing that many competing forces try to influence these decisions, those charged with making the difficult decisions remain faithful to the process of assuring that the final solution is in the long-term best interest of the district.

Omega School District followed this decision-making process as it grappled with the tough issue of computer use in the district. Superintendent Howell initiated this rational process by declaring that a goal of the district should be the most efficient possible use of computers in the Omega School District. She then outlined an approach that consisted of forming a task force, studying all sides of the issue, and reporting recommendations within a specified time period. Consistent with the rational model, the appointed task force conducted an exhaustive review of the four major uses of computers in school districts, applying a common set of criteria to each application. Finally, the task force presented the recommendation that they thought was in the long-term best interest of the district. This recommendation was systematically reviewed by the power structure and presented to the board of education for formal approval.

Having used a rational approach to decision making, the Omega District took great pride in the outcome of its systematic efforts.

## External Environment

To educators, the external environment means the world outside the school district. It contains all of the various forces residing outside the organizational boundaries of the school system that seek to exert influence on the operation of the school. School PTO groups, community agencies, and special interest groups are examples of the external environment.

The rational model treats the external environment exactly as the label says: external. There is not a substantial mixing of the internal with the external. More precisely, the external environment interacts with the district only at the periphery of the organization's territory. It does not intrude during the internal decision making of the district, waiting instead to respond after decisions are made internally.

The rational model also assumes that the external environment acts in a stable and certain fashion. As the district considers the various options in a given issue, the community's views and responses can be anticipated. The stability and certainty of the external world contribute to stability within the rational organization.

Another stabilizing feature of the external world is its acknowledgment of the expertise of the school district to make its own decisions. Because school district officials are the ones professionally trained and selected to deal with school issues, those outside the organization see no need to interject their own expert advice. Official power to make organizational decisions is vested in school officials, and the external environment respects the professional skills of the district staff.

Within the rational view of organizations, the peaceful coexistence between the school district and the external environment can be attributed largely to the school district's ability to understand accurately the world beyond the organization. Being able to make sense out of the external environment minimizes the energy spent on worrying about what these outside forces might think, say, or do to upset the direction of the school district.

The external environment in the Omega School District example behaved in just such a rational way. It did not interfere with the internal decision making of the district regarding computers. When the community did react, the response was predictably in support of the district's recommendations, acknowledging the thorough and professional approach the district took in its deliberations. In short, the Omega District conducted business as usual. Although the district stole an occasional glance at the posture of the community, it felt confident that the rational process would prevail, resulting in community support of district recommendations.

## Teaching Process

If the instructional goals of the rational organization are to find their way to the district's classrooms, the goals must be supported by a clearly conceptualized framework containing the best of what research has to say about good teaching. The rational model demands clarity of goals and efficiency in the delivery of goals. Therefore, the rational school district insists on a conceptual framework that most efficiently guides instructional practice.

Similarly, once the conceptual framework has been carefully described, the rational school district insists on explicitly defined steps to achieve specified outcomes. Applying this assumption to the classroom level, after instructional objectives have been identified, the most efficient means for achieving these objectives need to be described with care. This standard set of best practices should be followed by all teachers charged with teaching the specified objectives. To do otherwise would lead to inefficiency and, therefore, reduced effectiveness.

Finally, the rational school district points with pride to the fact that policymaking in the district directly affects teaching, which directly affects learning. After all, virtually every instructional policy established by the board and the administration is designed to result in improved learning by students. To achieve this goal of improved learning, the teaching process within the rational model is assumed to be affected by the policies set forth by the district.

Omega School District is testimony to this natural link among policy, teaching, and learning. When the senior administrative team selected a computer curriculum to be implemented, the next step was to specify teaching strategies that best achieved the goals of computer literacy. Eventually teachers throughout the district will be evaluated on the efficiency with which they deliver the curriculum by the performance of their students on tests reflecting the instructional objectives. If a formal evaluation reveals that the current program is not efficiently achieving its goals, the board may choose to modify policy, which could likely change the teaching strategies and correspondingly improve student learning.

## CONCLUSION

Admittedly, the organizational model portrayed in this chapter is characterized by rationality in its purest form. But even in a less extreme version, the rational model we have described has met with serious challenges of its ability to explain reality. Clearly, in the past, educational policymakers have acted as if the world was rational. But now the assumptions of rationality are under attack. Emerging from the rapid fire attack on rational systems is a growing consensus that, in general, the world in which schools exist is not rational and school district organizations, in particular, can't be described using the rational model. In Chapter 3, we apply the same dimensions used in this chapter to take a closer look at an emerging view of reality: nonrational educational systems.

# 3

# An Emerging View of Reality: Nonrational Educational Systems

_____

_____

_____

_____

_____

## INTRODUCTION

In Chapter 2 we argued that rational behavior is logical behavior with clear connections between goals, organizational structures, activities, and outcomes. What, then, is nonrational? In the most succinct sense, nonrational implies something other than rational, just as intuition and faith represent alternatives to rationality. In other words, nonrational doesn't necessarily mean irrational. Related to organizational life, nonrational behavior usually manifests a weak relationship among goals, structures, activities, and outcomes. Describing educational organizations as nonrational systems offers a competing view of reality. This perspective gains clarity as we examine another hypothetical study. This time we observe how the Delta School District employs a nonrational model in dealing with computer-related decisions.

## THE DELTA SCHOOL DISTRICT STUDY

In November 1983, Superintendent Howard Bale called the senior administrative team together for an important meeting. A condensed version of the meeting is described below.

Superintendent Bale began the meeting by asking Assistant Superintendent Donna Grange to review current policy regarding computer applications in schools.

Grange knew in advance the purpose of the meeting, and she had come well prepared. Still she appeared uneasy as she tried to reconstruct policy for the team.

Well, as you know, we don't have a clearly defined policy for using computers in schools. Our Coordinator for Computer Technology, Maria Sanchez, works like crazy to stay on top of things. But the field keeps changing so fast, we find ourselves making a lot of mid-course corrections.

Anyway, about three years ago several schools began to purchase some Commodore Vic 20s out of their school accounts. In addition, school PTOs, scrambling to protect their children from being computer illiterate, bought a variety of computer brands, largely determined by the advice of well-intentioned parents within the school community.

Anticipating the potential of multiple, competing goals for computer use, we began immediately to form a representative group of staff, principals, and parents from across the district to set some districtwide direction. For starters, we tried to discuss the pros and cons of the major uses of computers in schools:

- computer-assisted learning,
- computer-managed instruction,
- computer literacy, and
- administrative applications.

The discussion quickly turned into disagreements, with schools understandably defending their own decisions. Some schools had already trained key teachers to work with kids in the area of computer programming. Other schools, having purchased computers with ample memory, had already sent teachers to workshops so they could launch a computer-assisted learning curriculum in mathematics and language arts. Still other schools had done nothing systematically with the machines because staff members weren't ready to do anything. Despite the differences, each school felt justified in the way computers were being used.

We're at a point now, however, where we need a district goal regarding computers. Federal money has become available to purchase 110 computers within the next eight months. People are understandably confused about the direction this district is heading in computers. Buying over a hundred new computers without district policy to guide our decision spells more ambiguity and confusion.

Superintendent Bale observed the group's uneasiness as silence blanketed the room. The team members fidgeted with whatever was at hand, waiting for someone to break the silence. Finally, the superintendent smiled wryly and said:

This isn't the first time we have been in a situation of arriving at goals partly to explain activities already under way. Remember the time we asked the board to approve career education as a goal because we had just been notified of receiving a large grant that we had applied for as a lark. And what about the time the board surprised us with a 4-3 vote to implement full-day kindergarten in the district simply because the state department was willing to fund the program and our additional revenue would be more than double the added costs we would incur. I'm sure you can think of other examples that departed from the traditional, rational model of decision making.

Anyway, returning to the topic of computers, what are our options?

Assistant Superintendent Grange spoke up:

Realistically, our options are limited. Even though we probably should engage in a systematic process to determine the highest priority application for computers, we're too far down on the road to turn back. About 70 percent of our schools are emphasizing computer literacy while the rest who are using computers have concentrated on computer-assisted learning. To capitalize on the energy already expended, I feel we should give schools the latitude to pursue either or both of these goals.

Superintendent Bale agreed with this conclusion and he added:

Our district philosophy for some time has been to empower the schools with the ability to mobilize resources in order to achieve the goals they considered most important. In this situation, attention to computers is not going to disappear as quickly as some other innovations; open education, for example. What we need to do is gain board support for the twin goals of computer literacy and computer-assisted learning, then provide the necessary information, support, and resources to assist the schools in achieving these goals.

Subsequently, Bale asked Grange to reconvene the committee, develop a rationale for the two goals, and present these recommendations to the board within two weeks.

Because of prolonged discussions over the upcoming budget, the board postponed the agenda item on computers for five weeks. A decision had to be submitted before that time to the federal government regarding how the district would be using the 110 newly purchased computers. So the district assumed that it would be safe to declare both goals, computer literacy and computer-assisted learning, as part of district policy.

In the meantime, the board had been besieged by individuals and computer user groups lobbying for computer literacy to be the only goal of the district, at least for the present.

When it came to decision time, the board meeting room was packed. Seven separate computer user groups from the community turned out en masse to argue vehemently for literacy as the goal. Similar support was also evident from the university contingent. Assuming a much more low key profile, representatives from several PTO groups politely asked the board to consider computer-assisted learning as a district goal.

Debate, emotional appeal, and some displays of temper from community and board members filled the crowded room that evening. In the end, the board voted 4-3 against Superintendent Bale's recommendations. Instead they approved the single goal of computer literacy, even as one board member accused fellow members of "caving in" under pressure from the special interest factions. The next morning the superintendent convened the senior administrative cabinet once again.

Now that the decision has been made, we have an obligation to assist our teachers to implement the computer literacy goal. What sort of staff development activities should we consider?

Grange reminded the team that schools had different models of computers, requiring different types of training for teachers. She added:

Plus the literature on effective strategies suggests multiple ways to achieve the same goals. Therefore, I suggest we stay true to our school-based model and empower schools to determine the staff development needs most appropriate for their teachers. We will provide assistance as necessary to help them reach their goals.

The team accepted this recommendation, and the superintendent spent the balance of the meeting working with the team to develop an action plan for implementation.

A week later, the local newspaper conducted a reader poll to assess the community's long-range expectations for computer technology. Seventy-three percent of the respondents answered "yes" to the question: "Do you think the need for computer programming skills will be obsolete in five years?" Eighty-two percent said "yes" to the question: "Do you feel that using computers as a learning tool in a variety of subject areas will be the most important skill five years from now?"

Faced with this new information, the board felt an obligation to reconsider its initial position on computer goals. A month later, well after the staff training program for computer literacy had been launched, board members still had not voted on the motion to reconsider their original decision. Other, more urgent matters such as approving the annual budget laid claim to their attention.

## NONRATIONAL SYSTEMS

Like the Omega School District example, the Delta District scenario does not depict an actual district in action. However, it symbolically represents untold instances of educational organizations functioning in a nonrational world. Although the characters and script are different from the Delta dilemma, school districts throughout the country will likely identify with the nonrational view of real life in the organization. Again, a caveat is in order: nonrational does not mean nonsensible. The events and decisions we have just described do make sense and are understandable. However, to understand and make sense of Delta's experience, a conception of school districts as nonrational systems is more illuminating and more helpful than a rational conception.

The central difference between the two models lies in their interpretation of reality. Proponents of the rational model believe that a change in procedures will lead to improvement in educational practice. In short, the rational model begins with an "if-then" philosophy. If A happens, then B will logically follow. When reality fails to validate this "if-then" perspective (i.e., when B doesn't happen), the argument shifts to an "if-only" position. If only schools will tighten up rules and regulations, improved discipline will follow. If only teachers are given clear directives, then improved teaching will follow. Advocates for the nonrational model claim that the "if-then and if-only" model is wishful thinking; organizations do not always behave in a logical, predictable manner. Acknowledging this reality, the nonrational model attempts to turn it to the advantage of those in the system. Rather than spending organizational energy trying to conform to wishful thinking, the nonrational model allows us to invest our energy into devising solutions that will work, given reality.

To illustrate the nonrational model in more detail, we refer to the Delta School District study as we apply the same five criteria used in the rational model for examining organizations.

## Organizational Goals

Like the rational model, the nonrational model endorses the concept of organizational goals, but assigns a different meaning and importance to the construction of these goals. Both views of reality would argue that school districts do have a central mission: to improve learning and the quality of life in schools. When it comes to translating this mission statement into organizational goals, the nonrational and rational schools of thought part company.

For instance, the board of education may have a long list of district goals as part of board policy. Individual schools could have their own list, and certain parent organizations may produce still another list they want the school or district to address. The key, within the nonrational model, is to use organizational energy optimally in serving a variety of legitimate goals across different lists—as long as the district adheres to the overall mission of the organization.

Not only does the real world offer up multiple lists of organizational goals to be reckoned with, it couches these goals in ambiguous terms. As illustrated through the Delta School District example, the organization spends almost as much time defining and redefining as it does in actually implementing the goals. In many instances, goals are developed after the fact in an effort to make sense out of previous actions or to justify a particular course of action. According to the nonrational view, this behavior is understandable as the organization seeks meaning and clarity in a system disposed toward ambiguity.

These packages of multiple, ambiguous goals don't originate from a single source. Competing forces, in and out of the system, struggle to foist their agenda, their goals, upon the organization. Generally, these interest groups initially attempt to work within the district power structure to win their case. If unsuccessful through the traditional decision-making structure, they turn to other sources of policymaking. When the school district seems unwilling to teach basic skills, for example, the aggrieved group turns to the state legislature for mandated proficiency testing. Or, when the school district fails to adopt the goal of desegregation, the federal courts step in. The result is a laundry list of competing and sometimes conflicting organizational goals (Wise 1983).

Inevitably, organizational decision makers attempt to mediate these conflicting perspectives, but the system typically attends to selected goals at the expense of others. However, the nonrational model maintains that conflicting goals can be met. For instance, they don't have to be pursued simultaneously. Conflicting goals can be addressed in sequence, even though this approach won't satisfy all constituencies. As an illustration, a district may decide to focus on computer literacy next year, postponing implementation of a talented and gifted program until the new computer plan is in place. Also competing goals can be addressed by various units in the organization—the personnel department and the curriculum department could likely identify different areas needing attention. Rarely do we find occasions where school district goals are pursued in unison by all departments and schools in the organization. Instead, the school district moves along multiple fronts in its pursuit of organizational goals.

Just when the organization mobilizes resources to achieve selected goals, the goals may change. Over 20 years ago, Corwin (1965) challenged existing theory by asserting that organizational goals are in a constant state of flux as the school district resists, bargains, and adjusts to competing pressures, both within and outside of the organization. Whereas the rational model explains away these disturbances in the system or classifies them as evidence of poor management, the nonrational model acknowledges that this is the way the real world operates.

Finally, organizational goals often bear little resemblance to what happens in the classroom. Wise (1983) offers one explanation for this weak relationship:

The policymaking system shares few variables in common with the operating system. Indeed, the different actors in the education scene hold different ideologies and believe in different theories of education. Policymakers create policies which are consistent with the rational model and which would work if the rational model were a good representation of school reality. Practicing educators do not believe in the rational model and do not share its assumptions. The policies do not work because the rational model is incorrect (p. 108).

Lortie's research (1975) corroborates Wise's position. Lortie concluded that the formal goals of the school system have little impact on the actions of teachers. Specifically, he found that fewer than one third of the teachers he interviewed emphasized group achievement results (a district goal) as an indicator of successful teaching. This does not mean that organizational policy cannot influence teaching practice. It simply means that such influence isn't readily apparent or easily accomplished in the real world of school systems.

In the pretend world of Delta School District, Assistant Superintendent Grange began an important meeting by acknowledging that the district did not have a clearly defined policy for using computers in schools. She also forecast that multiple, competing computer goals loomed on the horizon, but the district failed in its attempts to head off a showdown. In the face of conflict, the superintendent of schools tried to strike a compromise solution by recommending dual goals: computer literacy and computer-assisted learning. Not surprisingly, however, various participants in and out of the district lobbied strongly for their favorite goal. The school board acceded to the pressures of the strongest interest groups by adopting computer literacy as the single goal. Then, just when the organization geared up to train teachers in the area of computer literacy, the board began to waffle on its decision. They voted to reconsider the possibility of computer-assisted learning as a district goal.

The experiences gained in the hypothetical world of the Delta District send important messages to the real world of school districts. Nonrational reality can't be contended with in strictly logical ways. A new paradigm is needed to handle effectively the multiple, competing, ambiguous, and changing goals of organizational life.

## Power

As stated in Chapter 2, power is the ability to mobilize energy in a school district to achieve the mission of improved learning and the quality of life in schools. In nonrational systems, the basis for power rests with the acquisition of three commodities: information (e.g., data, technical knowledge, exper-tise), resources (e.g., money, human services, material goods, space, time), and support (e.g., endorsement, backing, legitimacy). Attainment of these powerful commodities does not come automatically with the ascribed author-ity of a position. Anyone within the nonrational organization has the potential to get and use these sources of empowerment.

As more people are empowered, the organization grows and develops in its potency to achieve its mission. Therefore, in the nonrational view of reality, power units are not a fixed quantity: the number of people with a supply of power units can expand indefinitely, limited only by the amount of energy the system can safely absorb at any time, without overloading the circuits. The organization benefits from this open-ended interpretation of empowerment, as more people can contribute to the mission of the district.

Does it matter who is empowered? Yes, because the ultimate reason for mobilizing energy in the first place is to affect children's learning. De-centralization of decision-making power places the clout to make things happen as close to the action as possible. Numerous research studies con-verge on the theme that access to information, resources, and support by those ultimately responsible for using a specific innovation is critical to successful implementation (e.g., Berman and McLaughlin 1978 and Fullan and Pomfret 1977). Since implementation of programs happens most often at the school and classroom level, the nonrational model points to this level in the organization as the locus for real empowerment to be optimally effective.

Another argument for decentralized empowerment stems from the be-lief that school districts are loosely coupled systems (Weick 1976). Put suc-cinctly, looseness is described in relation to the likelihood that a change in A will rapidly produce a change in B. In a loosely coupled school district hierarchy, levels are relatively independent of each other. Each routinely makes decisions affecting operations within its own level with a minimal amount of control from the levels above. Actually, in addition to directives from the top not always being carried out precisely as ordered, often informa-tion from below isn't conveyed back up the hierarchy (Rubin 1983). For instance, teacher dissatisfaction with district policy mandating a particular teaching model may never reach the policymakers. Instead, teachers likely will adapt, even distort, the model to fit their needs. The nonrational model concludes that the reality of loose coupling reinforces the need to view decentralized empowerment as the most effective way to make a difference in classrooms.

Success in nonrational systems is measured by the ability to mobilize energy to get things done in an effective way. The watchword is not so much product as *process.* If an individual develops and implements a new program or organizes an innovative process for achieving an organizational goal, he or she gets recognized through added empowerment opportunities. Access to the basic empowerment commodities is not confined to the ascribed power positions. An organizational member's ability to draw on the counsel of senior administrators, build on the recognition of peer acceptance, and maintain alliances with subordinates creates an ascendency cycle. By mobilizing resources, an employee can make things happen, which strengthens credibility, which allows for more empowerment opportunities, which paves the way for more things getting done.

Superintendent Bale of the Delta School District recounted to the senior administrative team that the long-standing district philosophy was to empower the schools with the ability to mobilize energy to achieve their goals. This happens, he said, by providing the necessary information, support, and resources to assist the schools. When the board seemingly made a decision regarding district direction, the senior administrative staff supported multiple paths to achieving the goal, granting school personnel the latitude to determine how best to meet their students' needs. This latitude runs the risk that some schools will demonstrably not be as successful as others. The risk can be minimized through a carefully designed monitoring process governing major school decisions. The success stories will be highly visible, adding to the school's credibility and putting them in advantageous positions for future opportunities to demonstrate their empowerment prowess.

## Decision Making

Decisions assume center stage in any model of organizations. Particularly, policy formulation attracts attention because major policies commit the organization to define (or redefine) goals, establish strategies, and in general determine the long-range destiny of the organization (Baldridge and Deal 1983). Decisions are also the arena through which individuals and groups increase the probability of achieving their objectives. But final decisions don't tell the whole story.

The decision-making process in the nonrational model bears close scrutiny. Since logic doesn't always prevail in the nonrational world, the decision-making process, at times, may not produce decisions in the best interest of the organization. As described earlier in this section, the goals of an organization often are shaped by competing forces operating in restless coexistence until conflict looks likely. Then power struggles, bargaining, and compromise produce goals that don't conform neatly to the long-term destiny of the organization.

An understanding of goal formulation is important here because the decision-making process invariably gets linked to the goals of the organization.

In the nonrational model, decisions to be made don't coincide with the most important issues facing the organization. Instead, a problem gets flagged as needing a decision according to the myriad forces making the most claims on the organization's attention. Sometimes the squeaky wheel does get the grease. Other times an issue gets starred for attention because it offers a path of least resistance. On occasion, the problem receiving attention actually is the most important issue facing the school district at the time. But the safest prediction is that the most important problem gets defined as the most pressing one.

The decision-making process in the nonrational model doesn't conform to the neat, linear format inherent in the rational world. A wide variety of factors comes into play as final decisions are sought. Just as forces competing for organizational energy help shape issues receiving attention, individuals face competing claims for their own time. Most participants in the decision-making process juggle too many balls in the air at any given moment. Along with the various professional responsibilities jockeying for position, personal demands eat away at the physical and psychic energy on the job. In effect, full-time employees of the organization turn out to be part-time participants in any given decision-making process.

Most of the time, decision-making participants outside the organizational structure also perform this role on a part-time basis. They have more leeway, however, to move in and out of the decision-making process without feeling accountable for their spotty participation. In sharp contrast, at times the dogged persistence of outsiders dominates the decision-making process because they can devote full time, even overtime, to an issue about which they feel strongly. They learn quickly the meaning of the slogan, "Persistence pays off." Suppose, for example, a school community strongly contends that the children in grades one and two should ride a school bus because the parents consider the walking route to be too hazardous for that age group. Even though the school board has mixed emotions about the danger of walking to and from this particular school, after six successive appearances by parents at school board meetings plus a letter-writing campaign, topped off by a newspaper editorial supporting the parents' position, the school board decides that it's not worth $3,000 to continue the ongoing arguments. They vote to approve the $3,000 bus run. Persistence paid off.

The time frame for action plays an important role in how decisions get made. According to the nonrational model, the longer a choice remains unresolved, the greater the potential range of issues that are defined as relevant (March and Olsen 1976). Also, the longer it takes to reach a decision, the greater the potential number of participants who are activated. Therefore, if the decision-making process drags on, more issues tend to be dredged from the depths, and more participants get dragged into the process, complicating the decision-making process far beyond initial intentions.

Another source of pressure interrupting the smooth flow of decision making emanates from the external environment. As discussed more fully in the next section, external pressures insert stimuli into the process, causing the organization not only to respond but to accommodate these stimuli in order to get on with the decision-making process.

By the time all the political, economic, and social forces come into play, the organization frequently is left with a limited number of options for serious consideration. Unlike the rational model with its full house of options open and available to the decision makers, nonrational reality paints a smaller picture, with fewer choices to make and occasionally with the best choices already removed from the picture.

When decision time arrives, its advent is greeted with mixed emotions. Veterans of decision making in nonrational systems claim the final decision often emerges from a rush of last-minute negotiations, compromises, and concessions. Operating from a limited number of options brought forward for final deliberations, then having to bargain on these reduced choices, decision makers often aren't overly exuberant over the final outcome. Even though they strive to achieve the best possible outcome for the organization, they end up at times with decisions whose consequences don't have a strong correlation to initial intent. For example, major issues such as school closings, desegregation, school boundary changes, and large budget cuts don't always produce outcomes that are directly related to the intended purpose of serving kids better.

Delta School District chose to skip the formal decision-making process of considering all of the possible options for using computers and selecting the best approach for the district. They knew, realistically, that because of past practice and current expenditure restrictions the options were limited to computer literacy and computer-assisted learning. When they tried to convene a broad-based committee to study the issue, competing forces aborted the intended systematic approach, so the district chose a more political tack. They presented the board with only two options for consideration, both of which enjoyed a base of political support.

The board delayed a decision on the subject because of more pressing business. When board members finally got around to considering the issue, numerous political factors shaped their decision, with the final verdict determined more by politics than goals. But the final decision was not final. Board members found themselves pressure to reopen the decision-making process. At last report, the time frame for final action still was not resolved.

## External Environment

The nonrational model devotes a great deal of space to explaining the significance of the external environment in the internal affairs of the organization. The rational view of reality behaves as a closed system, not inviting the external world to participate until the closed loop of decision making is completed. Nonrational reality admits this would be nice, but in practice the choice is not usually an option for the organization to consider. The external environment maintains a high level of involvement in school district business. This involvement can be justified on a variety of grounds. But justification aside, in the nonrational model a highly charged environment will almost always be there. Sometimes, it may appear that the collective battery is running low. But, just when the organization starts taking the outside world for granted, sparks start flying, and "activated" becomes an understatement for describing the environment's relationship to the school district.

If the organization could predict the outside actors with some regularity, then planning could take into account their behavior. But the world outside the school district is filled with an assortment of full-time and part-time participants, each surfacing as the issues affect them directly then going underground temporarily, only to resurface when the occasion calls for it.

Because of this fluidity of participation, the external environment behaves in an unstable and often uncertain manner. Sustained leadership from the community is not likely because most participants from the outside are part-timers, and they speak only for a narrow constituency. They see their pet issue to a conclusion, then exit for awhile. With new issues, new participants arrive on the scene, carrying different baggage from previous visitors to the organization's world. Without a consistent set of values holding together the environment's expectations for the school district, the district proceeds to plan, knowing full well that instability and uncertainty caused by the external environment could result in the best laid plans going astray.

If predictability of external actors is problematic, the nonrational system would at least hope for certainty regarding when the nonpredictable behavior would occur. Such is not the case in the real world, however. The external environment intervenes in district business at virtually every opportunity (although the external actors would argue that it's their business, too). When considered necessary, actors in the external environment will inform the district of major problems needing attention, and then fade into the background, leaving the district and other part-time participants from the outside to struggle with the problem. On other occasions, when persistence seems necessary, the external environment actively sticks to the district task at hand until final decisions are made.

Life would be less complicated in the nonrational world if the external environment presented a uniform, coherent picture of reality. To the contrary, the nebulous thing called external environment hides behind multiple and shifting versions of reality. To the extent the school district can understand the environment, the district can plan accordingly. But the external environment can't be wrapped neatly in one package. For example, one version of reality for a professional, upwardly mobile community is an image of support, expertise, and social maturity for the school system to count on. The image may shift dramatically when the school district attempts to comply with court-ordered desegregation. Suddenly, the image of the community takes on a character of racist, territorial, and self-serving behavior to lobby for immunity from integration, quite a contrast from its previous image when turf and values were not threatened.

It didn't take long for the external environment in the Delta School District to intervene in the district business of making decisions about computers. In fact, community involvement in purchasing computers for the schools contributed to the multifaceted approach to computer use across the district. Once the community invested money in computers for selected applications, they developed ownership in seeing that these expectations were carried out.

The Delta environment became particularly active when the district tried to press for a decision on the most appropriate use of computers. Many latent, part-time participants in the community quickly rallied around their favorite use early enough in the decision-making process to be instrumental in shaping the (tentative) final decision. When the smoke cleared on the night of the emotional public hearing on computers, the board was swayed by the strong sentiment expressed for computer literacy as the number one goal of the district.

Two weeks later, conditions changed in the outside world. A local newspaper reported widespread community support for computer-assisted learning as a priority. "Facts" in hand, the board responded to the community by reopening the case.

## Teaching Process

Educators in the nonrational world reluctantly admit that the profession has failed to deliver an instructional technology that produces improved learning for all students or a single method guaranteeing an improved quality of life in schools. One reason for the reluctance is that this type of admission carries with it an acknowledgment of some inefficiencies of operation, which is anathema to the rational world view. In other words, if we don't have a single conceptual framework to guide educational practice, we run the risk of some meandering. Reality dictates, however. The nonrational model refuses to hide beneath a veil of absolute certainty if certainty doesn't exist. In the wake of this uncertainty, nonrational school districts grant the latitude for schools and teachers to continue their quest for a framework that fits with their respective interpretation of how children learn best in that school's context.

This latitude leads to a variance in goals across schools. Recalling from Chapter 1 the data about the diversity and complexity of today's student population, it makes sense to support a healthy measure of local autonomy in identifying those goals most appropriate to a particular student population within the limits established by the mission and current organizational goals of the district.

Consistent with local latitude in determining school goals, the nonrational model supports a multiple array of practices to achieve these goals. According to advocates for nonrationality, no evidence exists of a one best way to teach kids. The most effective teaching strategies depend on a complex set of factors, including the nature of the child's learning style, the context, and teaching style.

Finally, the nonrational model contends that policymaking bears little relationship to teaching and learning. In a loosely coupled system, policy decisions may create a large wake on the surface, but subside to a small ripple effect when finally reaching the school and classroom. Fault doesn't lie with the system, according to nonrational proponents. If blame is to be levied, it rests with the failure of policymakers to understand reality. Given a clear conceptualization of the nonrational model, policymakers can, in fact, design policies that contribute to improved teaching and learning. The key is understanding what can make a difference. Policies designed to mandate specific teaching strategies don't work, as described in detail throughout this chapter. Policies designed to facilitate decentralized decision making and expand empowerment opportunities to those closest to the action can make a difference. For example, a school board could decentralize decision making with a policy giving local schools greater control over the use of resources in the areas of personnel, curriculum, and instruction. The policy serves to empower teachers as they make important instructional decisions at the school and classroom level.

In subtle ways, the Delta School District reflected the nonrational view of the teaching process. Schools were permitted to experiment with different types of computers for different purposes. When decisions had to be made regarding district direction, the superintendent was willing to grant the latitude for schools to consider either computer literacy or computer-assisted learning (or both). Further, he went on record as supporting the necessary staff training to achieve these goals, recognizing that this training may take a variety of forms depending on the goal of the school and the specific staff development needs identified by the teachers. In summary, the Delta School District struck a balance between centralized dictation of *the one way* to teach computing in schools and the other extreme that *anything goes*.

# CONCLUSION

As cited in Chapter 2, numerous typologies have been constructed to describe and understand organizations. This chapter has outlined the nonrational view of school districts. Although the nonrational model departs from traditional ways of thinking about organizations, proponents argue that such a conception is more accurate than the rational model in portraying the reality of life in school districts. Baldridge and Deal underscore this shift in thinking as they contrast the theory prevalent in their 1975 book, *Managing Change in Educational Organizations,* with their more recent volume, *The Dynamics of Organizational Change in Education* (1983). According to the authors:

> Most notably, organization theory has relaxed its assumptions of rationality. Earlier theories emphasized logical connections between goals, structures, activities, and outcomes. People were seen as rational actors whose behavior would and should be guided by what was best for the collective welfare. But one by one, these assumptions have been called into question by substantial evidence that there may be a gap between theoretical "truth" and organizational "facts."
>
> As the experience of changing organizations began to accumulate, it soon became apparent that people and organizations are not very rational—or at least that they operate from a logic very different from that of theorists and administrators (p. 7).

Those holding a nonrational view realize the risks of being labeled "nonrational." The label can be misconstrued to mean irrational, connoting hopelessness and despair. Clearly, this chapter has painted a different picture, one that describes a world open to growth and change. It would be a gross misrepresentation and abuse of the nonrational model to use the label as an excuse for not taking deliberate action to improve education. Imagine the potential of comments such as, "Well, that's the nonrational world for you. We can't do much about it," or "The school board behaved nonrationally again—no wonder a responsible decision wasn't made." To put it bluntly, the label nonrational should not be a scapegoat for an honest attempt at describing reality. In fact, as we shall see in the next chapter, nonrational may turn out to be more realistic, after all.

# 4

# Is the Nonrational Model More Reasonable?

_____

_____

_____

_____

_____

## INTRODUCTION

As documented in previous chapters, the rational model continues to be the dominant framework for explaining how educational organizations operate. And, although many educators will argue that this is the way school districts should function, our intent is not to debate what ought to be but to describe how school districts, as organizations, do function.

To illustrate, even dramatize, the operation of school districts, we have chosen to construct two competing views of reality in educational organizations. In Chapters 2 and 3, we contrasted the rational and nonrational models along five dimensions as shown in Figure 4.1. We realize many variations exist on the theme, leading to other interpretations of reality. We also realize that no single paradigm withstands the test of the _one best way_ to describe all organizations under all conditions. In fact, as stated previously, most organizations are described by a reality that falls somewhere between the two extremes drawn in the previous chapters. After fully acknowledging that life in school districts isn't as pure as the competing models suggest, we contend nevertheless that the nonrational model generally portrays a picture of reality

## Fig. 4.1. Rational and Nonrational Models Contrasted

| RATIONAL | NONRATIONAL |
|---|---|
| **Goals** | **Goals** |
| • There is a single set of uniform goals that provides consistent direction for us. | • There are multiple, sometimes competing sets of goals that attempt to provide direction for us. |
| • The district goals are clearly stated and specific. | • The district goals are somewhat ambiguous and general in nature. |
| • The goals remain stable over a sustained period of time. | • The goals change as conditions change. |
| • Organizational goals are set via a logical, problem-solving process. | • Organizational goals are arrived at through bargaining and compromise. |
| • The goals for the district are determined by the leaders of the organization. | • The goals for the district are set by many different forces, both in and out of the organization. |
| **Power** | **Power** |
| • The formal organizational chart determines who can have power to make things happen. | • Having access to information, support, and resources is the basis for power to make things happen. |
| • Power to make things happen is located almost exclusively at the top of the organizational chart. | • Power to make things happen is located throughout the organization. |
| • There is a very direct connection between what the central office says should happen in the classroom and what actually goes on behind the classroom door. | • The extent of implementing central office directives is in large part controlled by teachers at the classroom level. |
| **Decision Making** | **Decision Making** |
| • The issues that receive attention are those which are most important at a given point in time. | • The issues that receive attention are those which are pressing for immediate resolution. |
| • The decision-making process makes sure that all feasible options are considered. | • The decision-making process usually ends up with a limited number of options to consider, constrained by factors such as politics, economics, and finances. |

| RATIONAL | NONRATIONAL |
|---|---|
| • The decision-making process keeps away extraneous forces (e.g., competing demands, outside pressures) that negatively affect logical decision making. | • The decision-making process accommodates various forces shaping eventual decisions (e.g., external pressures and persistence of people in their points of view). |
| • The decision-making process leads to a sound, one-best decision that maximizes organizational goals. | • The decision-making process incorporates compromise and concession, leading to a decision that may not have been the most educationally sound decision. |

**External Environment**

| RATIONAL | NONRATIONAL |
|---|---|
| • The environment external to the school district remains passive while organizational decisions are made internally. | • The external environment maintains an active level of involvement in organizational affairs. |
| • The external environment acts in a stable and predictable fashion. | • The external environment acts in a somewhat unstable and unpredictable manner. |
| • The external environment respects and defers to the official expertise and official power vested in school district staff. | • The external environment questions organizational expertise and challenges the power of school officials. |
| • The external environment acknowledges the right of the organization to make its own decision. | • The external environment demands a piece of the action at virtually every point in the decision-making process. |

**Teaching**

| RATIONAL | NONRATIONAL |
|---|---|
| • There is a clear picture of best instructional methods to achieve organizational goals. | • There is a somewhat fuzzy picture of best instructional methods to achieve organizational goals. |
| • There is a standard set of best practices to improve learning. | • There is a multiple array of effective practices to improve learning. |
| • School board policymaking directly affects teaching, which directly affects learning. | • School board policymaking bears very little direct relationship to teaching and learning in the classroom. |

in school districts that coincides with current research and accumulated experience (Baldridge and Deal 1983). Not only is the nonrational model a more accurate reflection of reality, it is a more sensible approach to organizational life in a world filled with change and uncertainty. We defend this point of view by referring once again to the five dimensions used to describe organizations.

# IN DEFENSE OF THE NONRATIONAL MODEL
## Goals

Organizational life would be simpler if goals were uniform, clearly stated, and stable over time. Efficiency would be greater if these goals were set by the leaders and translated into specific objectives by schools and teachers. But life isn't always so simple.

In reality, organizational goals are more accurately reflected in the nonrational column of Figure 4.1. Interpreted in the most pessimistic sense, this presents an image of a school district wandering aimlessly with no direction—a district at the mercy of the elements. A more realistic, less pessimistic interpretation depicts a district whose obligation and commitment is to serve a variety of diverse needs such as reflected in the data outlined in Chapter 1. More specifically, school districts are organized to serve multiple and sometimes competing goals, as various constituencies can legitimately claim their expectations should be met. It is possible, for instance, to have separate organizational goals that attempt to meet the needs of our talented students as well as those who are academically at risk—as long as these and other goals don't run contrary to the overall mission of the school district.

As another illustration, the fictitious Delta School District in Chapter 3 found that schools had various interpretations of how best to use computer technology. None of the interpretations were inherently good or bad. They simply reflected different, but reasonable, perspectives on what's best for students. The Delta District responded by trying to accommodate several of these goals. This approach allows the district to meet multiple obligations, as long as the goals don't pull the district in two opposite philosophical directions. When this condition surfaces, the district has a higher-order obligation: to lean on its guiding beliefs (see Chapter 5) to determine which direction is in the best interest of students.

Admittedly, at times organizational goals do become unnecessarily fuzzy, vague, and in direct competition with each other. Under these conditions, district leadership has an obligation to focus these disparate goals toward a common mission. At other times it's all right to have multiple goals that change over time as the organization demonstrates responsiveness to the diverse, pluralistic community it is designed to serve. It is also more democratic, especially in a public service institution. Finally, by incorporating different sets of goals, the district increases community support and commitment as more people have legitimate reason to become involved in district affairs.

## Power

The ability to mobilize energy within an organization stems from access to information, support, and resources. It follows, therefore, that the formal organizational chart does not inherently determine power. Those located at the top of the pyramid may be relatively more empowered, but this is because they understand the basis for power and they act on it. Others throughout the layers of the bureaucracy can gain access to the power tools, though it often takes more effort for the mid- to lower-level managers of the district. Organizations that accept the idea that empowerment can be an open-ended (as opposed to fixed) quantity also recognize that by increasing opportunities for empowerment organizational power is increased. Nevertheless, even under such positive conditions, some people will be more powerful than others, and this too is a reality of organizational life.

The rational model assumes that centralized expectations about curriculum and instruction travel downward through the organizational chart, showing up as intended in the behavior of teachers and students. The nonrational model denies this interpretation of reality, claiming instead that, in many instances, control over central expectations takes place at the school and classroom level. Furthermore, valuable ideas for district policy will often come from the schools and classrooms of the district if the channels of communication are open. Again, advocates of the nonrational model see this effect as more sensible. The power to make the most difference in the lives of children generally rests with those who are closest to these children. The reality of life in school districts is that teachers have considerable power to shape teaching and learning in the classroom.

## Decision Making

As shown in Figure 4.1, decision making in the rational model is based on setting goals via a logical, problem-solving process. This includes considering all feasible options within reach of the decision makers and arriving at the single best decision that maximizes organizational goals.

In the nonrational model, decision makers see this approach as not only unreasonable, but also undesirable. As discussed earlier, school districts serve multiple constituencies, each with legitimate demands and expectations. Organizational decisions, therefore, realistically are not confined to the inner circles of central administration. With some exceptions, an organization is forced to open the decision-making process to broad scrutiny and input, even if it means running the risk of having to contend with the politics of bargaining, compromise, and concession. Politics is not inherently dirty and devious. It simply reflects the reality of decision making in a democracy.

Exceptions to this general rule include decision making that *does* follow the tight coupling model. Within the business services side of the organizational chart, for instance, payroll and purchasing procedures usually follow the logical, decision-making process. Even on the instructional side chart, the logical, problem-solving approach works well for routine, noncontroversial decisions.

Another point of clarification needs to be made. Nonrational decision making doesn't mean irrational and irresponsible decision making. Even nonrational decision makers need to be analytical, systematic, and logical in their planning. But they know that many of the variables entering into the decision making don't follow the neat, orderly patterns assumed by the rational model. The trick is to design a decision-making process that anticipates, even incorporates, these variables in a sensible way.

## External Environment

Consistent with the neat and orderly world of rational organizations, the world of the external environment is just as rational. It acts in a stable and certain fashion, waiting patiently while the rational organization engages in internal decision making. Out of respect for the expertise and official power of the school district, the external world remains inactive until called on for a response.

Reality dictates otherwise, say defenders of the nonrational model. In this world of change and uncertainty, the environment external to the school district mirrors the conditions endemic to the larger society by acting in a somewhat unstable and uncertain manner. Such conditions aren't necessarily bad; they simply reflect the multifaceted and shifting versions of reality we live in.

Because those outside the school district have a stake in both the process and outcomes of schooling, they deserve to be included in the decision-making process of the district. This doesn't mean merely responding to internal decisions. It means becoming actively involved in the process itself, even to the point of challenging the organization's power and expertise. Although over 70 percent of our nation's families have no children in the public schools, they have an investment (both in a personal as well as societal sense) in the future of our educational enterprise. Therefore it seems reasonable that they should expect meaningful involvement in organizational decisions.

## Teaching Process

The teaching process within the rational world view presents a clear picture of the best instructional methods to achieve organizational goals. Correspondingly, there is a standard set of best practices to improve learning. If only teachers would put these practices into action in the classroom, teaching and learning would improve.

According to the nonrational model, things aren't quite that simple. The teaching process is a highly complex act, not easily understood by researchers or practitioners. Given the vast diversity among our student population, it seems only logical that teachers need an array of situationally appropriate instructional practices to improve learning. And, based on current research, the nonrational view of the teaching process turns out to be a more realistic perspective than the rational model.

## CONCLUSION

The rational view of reality has a lengthy history in our culture. In large part, the strength of the rational model emanates from a cultural aura that anything beyond the boundaries of rationality loses legitimacy. In fact, until recently, descriptions of reality that strayed outside the rational model were tossed into a residual category bearing no label.

Our attempt in this book is to describe reality in an analytical way, applying a framework commonly used in examining organizations. Although we have labeled this view of reality *nonrational,* the label should not become a distractor for the very important concepts subsumed under the label. To reiterate an earlier point, nonrational does not mean irrational. To the contrary, we argue that the nonrational model is a *more* sensible and *more* logical way of understanding the reality of organizations than the rational view. In addition, to be effective in a nonrational organization, leaders need to have an orderly, systematic, analytical approach to managing in a complex, somewhat disorderly environment.

The first step in creating school districts that work is to realize that the nonrational model does, indeed, offer a more logical and accurate account of how organizations actually operate. A next step is to put wheels under this model by developing specific strategies necessary to be effective in a nonrational world. In the next chapter we discuss the strategy of understanding and assessing the culture of the organization.

# 5

# Understanding and Assessing the Culture of the Organization

_____

_____

_____

_____

_____

_____

_____

_____

## INTRODUCTION

Thanks to the current outpouring of books on corporate reform, people are "discovering" that organizations have a culture. The fact is, they've always had a culture, but not many people in or out of the organization paid much attention to it. Today the culture of the organization has become a prominent factor in the study of what makes organizations tick (e.g., Deal and Kennedy 1982, Kanter 1983, Davis 1984, Miller 1984). More specifically, organizational culture becomes instrumental in determining organizational health. In the following section, we address questions such as, What is meant by "culture"? How do you know one when you see one? How do you assess the health of the organizational culture? How do you resolve differences between what is and what ought to be? For answers to these questions, we draw heavily on the research and experience of the business world.

## UNDERSTANDING ORGANIZATIONAL CULTURE

In an abbreviated way, culture can be defined as: the way we do business around here; who you are and what you stand for; the assumptions about the organization. In a more scholarly sense, culture embraces the norms, values, history—the sum total of all the shared understandings held by members of the organization. However, such a definition is too amorphous for purposes of describing and analyzing culture. Therefore, we operationally define culture along two dimensions: the guiding beliefs of the organization coupled with the day-to-day behavior of organizational members. Davis (1984) offers the caveat that beliefs and behavior are only manifestations of the culture, and not the culture itself. But, as he puts it, " . . . artifacts are tangible, and it is possible to get your arms around them" (Davis 1984, p. 12). With this caveat in mind, we examine more carefully each of the dimensions of culture.

## Guiding Beliefs

Rooted in a philosophical context, guiding beliefs are the principles on which the organization is supposedly built. Ideally, they serve as the foundation for all major decisions. For school districts, guiding beliefs provide direction in areas such as school board policymaking, allocation of resources, utilization of personnel, and for making critical decisions about teaching and learning. Sometimes guiding beliefs take the form of a mission statement, district philosophy, or goals and objectives. More frequently, guiding beliefs are embedded in stories about the history of the organization, various key documents shaping the direction of the district, and the verbal and nonverbal messages sent by the school board and senior-level administrators.

In any case, every organization conveys a belief structure that members of the organization interpret as representing the values held dear by those who are expected to set the tone and direction for the district: the school board and district administrators.

## Daily Behavior

The second dimension of organizational culture is the daily behavior of the employees of the school district. This component of culture is more situational and subject to change due to circumstances of the moment. Deal and Kennedy (1982) refer to this behavior as the rites and rituals of the organization. For example, subtle clues about behavior are found in the way people are addressed, how much emotion is permitted, who speaks out at meetings, and the acceptability of playfulness as part of organizational life. In short, the daily behavior of staff members reflects the way the school district does business on a continuing basis.

## Climate and Culture

At this point a distinction needs to be made between climate and culture. Climate is a measure of whether people's expectations are being met regarding what it should be like to work in the school district. These expectations plus the guiding beliefs produce norms that powerfully shape the behavior of individuals and groups in the organization. Climate, then, becomes the fit between the prevailing culture and individual values of employees (Davis 1984). Whereas climate is often transitory and a short-term phenomenon, culture is more stable and long term.

## Describing School District Culture

Once the idea of organizational culture takes on meaning to school district leaders, the ability to describe the culture of the district can be incorporated into organizational strategy.[1] This step is easy when the district has a clearly articulated set of guiding beliefs which is manifest in daily behavior by members of the organization. The rub comes when guiding beliefs are not so apparent. According to researchers in the corporate sector (e.g., Davis 1984, Miller 1984), the most effective way to uncover data about organizational culture is through interviews with key informants. "Key," in this case, means individuals who have a long history with the district and who have a broad, diverse background of experience with the organization. Basic categories for collecting information about the district culture (Hickman and Silva 1984) include:

• the district's history—events, decisions, and people who gave shape to the present organization;

• dreams, ambitions, and values of select employees, those who strongly influence other employees;

• organizational stories containing important messages about the district's priorities, commitment, concerns, star employees, dos and don'ts, as well as general ways of getting things done; and

• the performance, motivation, and relationships of the district's employees.

Leaders in the field of organizational culture contend that the step of describing the culture is a prerequisite to understanding and assessing the culture. The experts also prefer the interview process primarily because of the rich lore found in firsthand accounts. However, in cases where time, money, and other resources become major obstacles to describing the culture via interview, a written questionnaire can also yield valuable information.

Whether the organizational strategy is to interview, conduct a written survey, or a combination of methods, the data need to be organized according

---

[1] Note that the focus of this section is on *district* culture. Within each culture, subcultures exist and have their own norms, values, and history. See, for instance, Deal and Kennedy (1982). For a discussion of school culture as a subculture within the district, refer to Chapter 9.

to major principles. Since no single framework stands out in the literature as the preferred system, each district must group the guiding beliefs according to its own needs. To illustrate what a framework might look like, we have constructed in Figure 5.1 some typical categories along with sample questions related to each category.

### Fig. 5.1. Guiding Beliefs of Our School District

*Principle of Purpose*
To what extent does the district:

- articulate a set of purposes that provides long-term direction to the district?
- value the importance of employees understanding the purposes of the district's mission?
- value the importance of decisions being made with consideration to the purposes?

*Principle of Empowerment*
To what extent does the district:
- value empowering employees throughout the district to assist in the mission of the district?
- value equal opportunity to access information, support, and resources?
- view power as an expanding entity throughout the organization?

*Principle of Decision Making*
To what extent does the district:
- support the decentralization of decisions as close to the point of implementation as possible?
- value opportunity for input in districtwide decisions?
- value decisions being made by those who are directly affected by them?

*Principle of Belonging*
To what extent does the district:
- value commitment to the development of the individual within the district?
- treat individual employees as significant stakeholders in the organization?
- value a "we spirit" and feeling of ownership in the organization?

*Principle of Trust and Confidence*
To what extent does the district:
- believe that employees act in the best interest of students and the organization?
- have confidence in the expertise of staff members to make wise decisions?
- believe that employees will respond with their best efforts when appropriately recognized?

*Principle of Excellence*
To what extent does the district:
- value high standards and expectations?

- value an atmosphere encouraging all staff members to "stretch and grow"?
- believe in a "can do" attitude for all employees?

*Principle of Recognition and Reward*
To what extent does the district:
- value offering incentives to encourage innovation and risk taking?
- believe in recognizing employees and students who achieve significant accomplishments?
- believe in investing in the potential of district employees?

*Principle of Caring*
To what extent does the district:
- value the well-being and personal concerns of the employees?
- believe in employees sharing themselves in an open and trusting manner?
- value taking a personal interest in the professional development and career of employees?

*Principle of Integrity*
To what extent does the district:
- value honesty in words and action?
- value consistent, responsible pursuit of a stated course of action?
- value the unwavering commitment to highest personal and ethical convictions?

*Principle of Diversity*
To what extent does the district:
- value differences in individual philosophy and personality?
- value and encourage differences in teaching style and philosophy?
- believe that schools and the children within them are inevitably not alike, calling for flexibility in teaching and learning approaches?

A school district's culture moves from background to foreground when organizational strategies are employed that create an awareness of culture, underscore its importance, and systematically begin to describe it. These strategies can be applied to the guiding beliefs as well as to daily behavior.

The first dimension produces a measure of how things ought to be, and the second dimension yields a picture about how things really are.

# LONG BRANCH SCHOOL DISTRICT STUDY

The following hypothetical example illustrates how a new superintendent set about the business of understanding the culture he recently inherited. For the sake of brevity, only one guiding belief is highlighted: the principle of decision making.

Donald Harrington recently accepted the superintendency of Long Branch School District, a community with 12,000 students and 21 schools.

Harrington previously had spent six years as superintendent of a much smaller district about 55 miles southeast of Long Branch.

Harrington made it clear to the Long Branch Board of Education that he valued one principle very highly. He felt it was extremely important to decentralize decisions as close to the spot of implementation as possible. Similarly, he valued the opportunity for teaching staff to have input into districtwide curriculum and instruction decisions as much as feasible, even though he was firm that the superintendent and board should make the final decisions on those issues affecting the entire district.

Harrington was also seasoned enough to know that he couldn't walk through the crowds waving his banner and expect an immediate followership just because the superintendent was leading the pep rally. Instead, he decided to use a combination of interviews and a survey to better understand the Long Branch culture in the area of decision making.

First, he scheduled a series of three meetings over a month's period with each of four influential members of the district. The first person he selected was the director of personnel, who had been in the district for 21 years, serving in a variety of roles such as curriculum specialist, middle school principal, and team leader of the administrative negotiating team. The second person was the most experienced high school principal, considered a star by all accounts. She had previously been an assistant principal in two other high schools before accepting her current position in the district's most difficult high school. The third person he identified was the president of the teachers' union. Even though this person was a leader during the tough teachers' strike, she was an adamant supporter of children. She also understood the important role of management in the overall scheme of running a school district. The fourth person interviewed was a custodian who had been with the district for 27 years and had worked for nine different principals. He was acclaimed for his dedication to the Long Branch District. Besides, he was a savvy person when it came to understanding the various agendas that principals held in managing a school. From his several meetings with these individuals, Superintendent Harrington reflected on the following notes he had jotted down about decision making.

*The Long Branch District has consistently gone on record in various documents stating the importance of involving teachers in the development of curriculum.*

*Teachers believe the district wants to hear their ideas about what works best for kids.*

*Classified personnel don't seem to have any clear messages about whether the district values including them in decisions affecting their work life.*

*Administrators, in general, feel that the district doesn't value their input in district policymaking.*

*School board policy includes a paragraph about the importance of delegating decisions to those who are most affected by them.*

*Employees, except for teachers, don't see a lot of evidence that the school board acts according to the policy statement about delegation.*

*Teachers want to be involved in curriculum and instruction decisions, but not particularly in decisions in other areas such as bus schedules and redrawing school district boundaries.*

To complement the interview process, Superintendent Harrington sent out a brief report card to be anonymously filled out by all employees regarding their perceptions of school district operations. In the area of decision making, the following results were noteworthy:

*Question:* Do the district administration and board value your input in decisions?

*Response:* Teachers, 67 percent yes; administrators, 34 percent yes; classified staff, 29 percent yes.

*Question:* Does the district allow you to make decisions that affect you?

*Response:* Teachers, 81 percent yes; administrators, 41 percent yes; classified staff, 39 percent yes.

The survey tally fell in line with the firsthand data gathered by Harrington. He concluded, therefore, that the guiding belief of decentralized decision making was a value that at least was officially expressed by the district. This value was clearly one he endorsed. Harrington further concluded that the value wasn't uniformly understood as being important to district operations. Both district administrators and classified personnel weren't convinced that the value was considered important by the board and senior-level administrators. Finally, Superintendent Harrington realized that the daily behavior of district administration and the school board wasn't interpreted to be supportive of a decentralized decision-making policy statement.

Therefore, Superintendent Harrington made a commitment to strengthen the communication process so that all employees realized that the district did, indeed, value decentralized decision making. He also pledged to monitor the actions of key district staff to reinforce and recognize efforts to make the value of decentralized decision making come alive in the behavior of employees, particularly those in leadership roles, who serve as role models for others.

## ASSESSING THE HEALTH OF SCHOOL DISTRICT CULTURE

As Superintendent Harrington would quickly attest, ideally, the guiding beliefs should set the tone and direction for organizational strategies (i.e., the strategies should flow from the belief system). Correspondingly, the daily behavior of school district employees affects whether the strategies get implemented. If the culture is healthy, there should be a natural progression from guiding beliefs to organizational strategies to daily behavior. But if the guiding beliefs are not strong within the organization, daily behavior takes center stage (Davis 1984). Without guiding beliefs as anchor point, the everyday activities start to dictate organizational strategy. When this happens, the organization loses its future focus and becomes preoccupied with survival of the moment.

To summarize, a balanced equation occurs when the guiding beliefs equal the daily behavior (G.B. = D.B.). Assuming appropriate guiding beliefs, the outcome is a healthy culture. In contrast, when G.B. ≠ D.B., the result is an unhealthy culture. Deal and Kennedy (1982) offer additional symptoms of a culture in trouble:

weak cultures don't have clear values or beliefs about how to be effective; or

they have many such beliefs but can't agree among themselves on which are most important; or

different parts of the organization have fundamentally different beliefs; or

the heroes of the culture are destructive or disruptive and don't build upon any common understanding about what is important; or

the rituals of day to day life are either disorganized, with everybody doing their own thing—or downright contradictory, with the left hand not knowing what the right hand is doing (pp. 135–136).

## DEALING WITH DIFFERENCES BETWEEN WHAT OUGHT TO BE AND WHAT IS

To reiterate, the litmus test of the health of the organizational culture is the balance between what ought to be (guiding beliefs) and what currently exists (daily behavior). If an imbalance appears, several questions should subsequently be asked to diagnose the cause of the imbalance.

1. *Are the guiding beliefs still desirable?* If so, leave them alone. If not, a major change effort looms ahead. More about this later.

2. *Are the guiding beliefs desirable, but not clearly understood or, perhaps, misinterpreted?* In this situation, organizational strategies need to be developed that strengthen the official and informal communication networks, underscoring the importance of key values. Also recognition should be extended to events and people exemplifying these values.

3. *Are the guiding beliefs all right, but the daily behavior doesn't coincide with the values?* Then a slow, deliberate process needs to be implemented aligning the organizational structure, strategies, and skills with the professed values. In many cases, only a few areas of daily behavior may be out of balance, which makes the balancing act less formidable. Other times, a strategy may be to manage around the daily behavior. In particular, if the daily behavior is deeply entrenched, it may be more productive to tolerate the out of balance daily behavior while reinforcing the guiding beliefs (Davis 1984).

Returning to the issue of changing organizational culture, most experts agree that a decision to make drastic changes in the school district culture should be made only under the most serious conditions. That is, if the guiding beliefs contribute to a very unhealthy organization, then the risks involved in overhauling the culture may be worth it. What are the risks? The investment of time and energy in attempting to recast a form that has already hardened is one risk. Another is the probability that the resistant organizational culture will prevail, rendering the leader powerless.

A more promising approach is to build on the strengths of an organization's culture. Reinforce the guiding beliefs that are desirable. Identify the select few that need to be changed, and then develop organizational strategies for sending clear messages that the new guiding beliefs are extremely important to the leaders of the school district. Reward and remind at every opportunity the value of these new beliefs. Recall, for instance, that Superintendent Harrington in the Long Branch study improved the communication process so that all district employees heard the message about the importance of decentralized decision making. He also highlighted performance of district staff, which represented this value in action. Over time, the school district will see the pattern of leadership behavior calling attention to what's important within the organization's belief structure.

# 6

# Strategic Planning

## INTRODUCTION

Conventional planning models make things seem so easy. To be effective, administrators simply identify long-range goals, develop procedures to achieve the goals, and put together an evaluation design that will assess the achievement of the goals. But most administrators don't behave the way the planning models say they should. For instance, based on interviews with administrators, Baldridge (1983) reported the following patterns of administrative planning:

• Administrators move from one event to the next with little time for long-range planning.

• As soon as long-range goals start looking clear, something happens to muddle them up again.

• Instead of a crisp list of a few clear goals, real world administrators face a laundry list of unclear and sometimes contradictory goals.

• Rarely are long-range program decisions based on rational evaluation. Rather, a typically weak evaluation design is intertwined with the political support a program can muster.

• Even when a plan is made, it virtually never gets implemented as intended.

In short, the real world of administration does not coincide with the ideal world described by conventional planning models. To reconcile this gap, we concur with Baldridge and Deal (1983) that planning theory should be adjusted to reality, not reality forced into an obsolete theoretical framework.

# FOUNDATION FOR STRATEGIC PLANNING

Actually, there is a body of planning literature that does demonstrate a sensitivity to the real world of administration. Over the past 20 years, research in schools of management has sought to determine effective planning strategies. This literature has converged into a solid conceptual framework under the heading *strategic planning*.[1] The basic assumptions of strategic planning relate directly to the view of organizations developed in Chapter 3. The real world of school districts is best characterized by the nonrational model. In particular, two points stand out that have special meaning for planning. First, we believe in a dynamic world marked by rapid change. Any planning model should recognize and accommodate the dynamics of change. Second, the external environment is inextricably bound into our planning efforts. As described in Chapter 3, the environment will influence our decisions, so we need to incorporate data from this macroenvironment when we engage in the organizational strategy of planning.

According to Rhodes (1986), the simplest way to understand strategic planning is to view it as an information model:

Strategic planning parallels the process the human mind uses to make decisions in situations where conditions have changed since the last time a similar decision was made. At such times, when old assumptions may not be valid, the mind actively searches for new and better information. ("New" means information related to the *current* situation, and "better" means information more specifically related to the *purpose/outcome* of the decision.) Using this data a new decision is made. Its effects on the situation then produce new information for subsequent decisions. Using this analogy, strategic planning can be understood, simply, as a process that provides *new and better information* for decisions related to the immediate or future accomplishment of an objective (pp. 1–2).

---

[1] For those who are interested in tracing the roots of strategic planning, see Cope (1981).

The concept of linking present decisions to future objectives is a critical point. Planning within a context of changing conditions means that planners need a clear conception of the organization's mission. In the case of a school district, a carefully articulated vision of where the district is heading needs to be kept in the forefront of discussions as strategic planning processes are put in motion.

With the foundation for strategic planning established, let's contrast the framework of strategic planning with the more familiar framework of conventional, long-range planning.

# CONVENTIONAL VS. STRATEGIC PLANNING

In an attempt to highlight differences between conventional and strategic planning, Figure 6.1 illustrates two competing frameworks, with the full realization that the real world doesn't always fit an either-or model.

## World View: Internal vs. External

Consistent with the rational systems model, conventional planning takes into account only the variables operating within the system. The world of importance to conventional planners is the world of the organization. In contrast, strategic planners say the world of importance in planning comprises a dual environment: the world of the school district plus the external environment. According to Lewis (1983), recognition of the external environment as an important consideration in the planning process and actually using data derived from the environment are two essential features separating strategic planning and conventional planning.

## System Perspective: Segmental vs. Integrated

In a segmentalist system, each unit within the organization is self-contained, functioning independently of other units. Planning in such a system

**Fig. 6.1. A Comparison of Conventional and Strategic Planning**

| Category | Conventional Planning | Strategic Planning |
|---|---|---|
| World View | Internal | External |
| System Perspective | Segmental | Integrated |
| Planning Horizon | Long Range | Medium/Short Range |
| Data Base | Quantitative | Qualitative |
| Outcome | Master Plan | Masterful Planning |

tends to view these discrete units as responsible for their own destiny. In an integrated system, planning emphasizes interdependency, crosscutting relationships among organizational units, and the concept of the "whole" of the organization in planning efforts.

To illustrate these different perspectives, suppose a school board developed a district policy to "mainstream" special education students into regular classrooms as much as possible. In a segmentalist system the following scenario may unfold.

A central office administrator in special education hires the teachers with no input from principals. The special education teachers and classroom teachers plan their curriculum with little communication between each other. Academic and behavior problems in the special education class are the exclusive responsibility of the special education teacher. If serious behavior erupts from a given special education child, the principal calls the central office to see what the administrators in special education plan to do about "your kid."

In contrast, an integrated system perspective causes a different story to be told.

The central office administrator in special education works in cooperation with the building principal to interview and select a special education teacher. The classroom teachers and special education teachers set aside some common planning time so coordination of curriculum will be maximized for the students. Academic and behavior problems become the joint responsibility of the special education teacher, classroom teacher, and support staff, including the guidance counselor, school psychologist, and reading specialist. When major problems occur, both central office staff and the school operate from a perspective, "We're all in this business together, and we're dependent on each other to resolve issues in the best interest of the school district."

## Planning Horizon: Long Range vs. Medium/Short Range

What constitutes "long range" varies according to planning models; much of the conventional planning literature focuses on developing five-year plans, ten-year plans, even plans carrying the organization into the next century. Strategic planners aren't opposed to looking ahead. In fact, they would argue that the long-range destiny of the organization is crucial to effective planning. When it comes to actual planning horizons, though, the strategic planning framework rests on the assumptions of change and an active external environment. Because we are educating in an era of change and instability, we can't assume today's plans will meet tomorrow's needs. Also, realistically, involvement by the world outside the school district may cause us to see things in a different way, thereby altering our original plans. For these reasons, the planning timeline can be as short as a few days or as long as, perhaps, a couple of years.

## Data Base: Quantitative vs. Qualitative

Traditionally, planning models have relied on hard data because these figures offered the most defensible basis for making tough decisions about the future. Strategic planning models, on the other hand, emphasize qualitative data. Because the future is uncertain, subjective judgment, intuition, and even hunches become important pieces of data in planning for the future.

## Outcome: Master Plan vs. Masterful Planning

It seems almost too obvious to state, but the goal of conventional, long-range planning is to produce a long-range plan. This plan becomes the blueprint for organizational activities and decisions during the time period covered by the plan. Adherence to the plan means adherence to efficiency (i.e., doing things right as defined by the blueprint). An analogy will illustrate the concept of master plan. Imagine a maze puzzle designed for children. There is one entry point and one exit point, with the exit point representing successful execution of the plan. Contained within the maze is one right path to success. The exit point doesn't change, and the barriers along the way remain static. The challenge is to negotiate your way through the barriers and dead ends, knowing a right answer lies within your reach.

In contrast, the goal of strategic planning is to produce a stream of wise decisions designed to achieve the mission of the organization. Emphasis shifts from product to process. Just as the planning process builds in flexibility for adapting to changing conditions in and out of the organization, it also accepts the possibility that the final product may not resemble what was initially intended. In other words, strategic planners say it's okay to abandon some original goals that looked good at first. Substituting goals may not result in the most efficient planning, but it nets a more effective process because changes made today are designed to make the organization better off in the future.

To draw another analogy, imagine strategic planning in action as playing a video game. The mission is to score one million points. To achieve this level of excellence, the player negotiates a path packed with stimuli from the external environment trying to block the road to excellence. The player must make a stream of wise decisions en route, even changing some plans along the way, always on the alert for the unexpected. In this illustration, the most effective way to achieve excellence may not be the plan as originally intended at the outset of the game.

In summary, strategic planning is not some package that will produce magic results overnight. Rather, it offers a different way of thinking about planning in comparison to conventional, long-range planning. This change in orientation carries with it some techniques that will strengthen the strategic planning process.

# THREE NECESSARY TECHNIQUES FOR STRATEGIC PLANNING

Since this is not a book on everything you ever wanted to know about planning, we will skip the basics and move directly to three techniques requisite to an effective strategic planning process. Application of these techniques assumes that the organization already has in place a mission statement that serves as an anchor point for future planning.

## Environmental Analysis

As school districts plan in the real world, they quickly realize the importance of monitoring various aspects of their external environment. The trick becomes deciding what to monitor. By grouping data according to economic, political, technological, and social dimensions, many school districts find that this data base is sufficient for most purposes in environmental scanning. For each of these dimensions, the data can be further categorized according to two effects: opportunities and threats. Opportunities are areas in which favorable circumstances provide potential for help in achieving district goals. Threats represent potential problems that could have a serious negative impact on the district's attempts to achieve its goals (Lewis 1983). For each of the four dimensions of the external environment, (economic, political, technological, social) the following questions can be posed.

• What are the (e.g., economic) forces that serve as opportunities to help in the accomplishment of the planning issue?
• What are the (e.g., economic) forces that serve as threats to the accomplishment of the planning issue?

By collecting data that provide answers to these two questions along each of the four dimensions outlined above, a district can produce a rather comprehensive scan of its external environment. Figure 6.2 illustrates a sample format for an environmental analysis.

## Internal Analysis

For any issue a district subjects to strategic planning, an analysis can be made of the potential organizational impact of the issue. We have structured the internal analysis along three dimensions: educational impact, economic impact, and political impact. Figure 6.3 provides a sample format for an internal analysis.

## Integration of Environmental Analysis and Internal Analysis

After reviewing the quantitative and qualitative data available from the external world and the world of the organization, strategic planners pool this information to arrive at recommendations for action that are consistent with

### Fig. 6.2. Strategic Planning
### Environmental Analysis

*Planning Issue:* _____

*Dimension:* ECONOMIC
1. What are the economic forces that serve as opportunities to help in the achievement of (planning issue)?

2. What are the economic forces that serve as threats to the accomplishment of the planning issue?

*Dimension:* POLITICAL
1. What are the political forces that serve as opportunities to help in the achievement of (planning issue)?

2. What are the political forces that serve as threats to the accomplishment of the planning issue?

*Dimension:* TECHNOLOGICAL
1. What are the technological forces that serve as opportunities to help in the achievement of (planning issue)?

2. What are the technological forces that serve as threats to the accomplishment of the planning issue?

*Dimension:* SOCIAL
1. What are the social forces that serve as opportunities to help in the achievement of (planning issue)?

2. What are the social forces that serve as threats to achievement of the planning issue?

**Fig. 6.3. Strategic Planning
Internal Analysis**

*Planning Issue:* _____

1. What is the educational impact of this issue on the organization?

2. What is the economic impact of this issue on the organization?

3. What is the political impact of this issue within the organization?

the school district's guiding beliefs, economically justifiable, politically attainable, and educationally sound.

To provide a glimpse of one school district's application of the strategic planning process, we focus on a committee considering a full-day kindergarten program.

## WILDLIFE SCHOOL DISTRICT STUDY

As directed by the board of education, the Wildlife School District recently formed a committee to study the feasibility of implementing a full-day kindergarten program in the district. In the past, all kindergarten programs had been half day, with the exception of one full-day program financed by Chapter 1 funds. In approaching the planning process, the committee organized its activities into three steps: environmental analysis, internal analysis, and integration of the external and internal analyses. To avoid going into a lengthy description of the complete planning process, we will look at the economic and political dimensions as they relate to the full-day kindergarten decision.

### Environmental Analysis

In examining opportunities and threats, the committee dealt with the questions stated below.

*Question:* What are the economic forces that serve as opportunities to help in the implementation of full-day kindergarten?

*Data:* The state Department of Public Instruction had decided to reimburse school districts the equivalent of one half the average per pupil expenditure for each student enrolled in a full-day kindergarten program. For Wildlife, this meant about $2,000 per student or roughly $40,000 per kindergarten classroom. This revenue would more than offset the cost of paying for a 0.5 teacher position and necessary furniture and supplies.

*Question:* What are the economic threats in considering a full-day kindergarten program?

*Data:* If the state department withdrew funding, it could prove costly for the district in maintaining a full-day program strictly at district expense.

*Question:* What are the political forces that serve as opportunities to help implement full-day kindergarten?

*Data:* The local university is excited about the opportunity for a full-day program. They would have a lab for training student teachers, and they would have opportunities to conduct research on the effects of full-day kindergarten. Also, from a political perspective, many parents would welcome the chance for the district to assume full-day responsibility for their child instead of paying a babysitter.

*Question:* What are the political forces that serve as threats to implementation of full-day kindergarten?

*Data:* Some parents don't want to give up the half day of time they currently enjoy with their children. But these same parents don't want other children in the class having an undue advantage of being in school all day. So a contingent of parents will object to the full-day program on political grounds.

## Internal Analysis

The district identified three major alternatives for consideration: implement full-day kindergarten in all schools, implement full-day kindergarten in selected schools, or continue to implement only the half-day program.

ALTERNATIVE 1: Full-day kindergarten in all schools.

*Question:* What is the educational impact of this alternative?

*Data:* Every child would get an excellent start in school. Some teachers would not be trained to implement the more comprehensive, full-day program.

*Question:* What is the economic impact?

*Data:* The district would make money on the program, since revenues would exceed expenses.

*Question:* What is the political impact?

*Data:* Some teachers don't want the full-day program. They aren't secure in being able to handle the expansion into a full-day's worth of lessons. The board of education would have to change school boundaries because space would not be available in all schools to accommodate the program.

ALTERNATIVE 2: Full-day kindergarten in selected schools.

*Question:* What is the educational impact of this alternative?

*Data:* Some children would benefit by participating in a full-day program. Other children would be denied this educational opportunity.

*Question:* What is the economic impact?

*Data:* For each school offering a full-day program, the state department would reimburse the district accordingly. Therefore, the program would pay for itself.

*Question:* What is the political impact?

*Data:* Some schools would be considered as more desirable because they offered a full-day program. Selection of these schools could become a politically volatile issue.

ALTERNATIVE 3: Full-day kindergarten in no schools.

*Question:* What is the educational impact of this alternative?

*Data:* All children would be denied the opportunity to participate in a full-day kindergarten program.

*Question:* What is the economic impact?

*Data:* The district would not gain or lose financially if the full-day program were not implemented.

*Question:* What is the political impact?

*Data:* Many parents would be upset that their child did not have the opportunity to benefit from a full-day program. Other parents would be upset because they couldn't get the extra half day of child care. The non-supporters of a full-day program would be relieved that all children would be treated "equally" (i.e., a half day for everyone).

## Integration of Environmental and Internal Analysis

Weighing all of the data from the environmental analysis and internal analysis, the full-day kindergarten committee recommended implementation of the program at selected sites within the district, making it optional for students and maintaining the half-day program in all schools. The committee felt the combined assessment of the external and internal environment via a strategic planning model led them to a very sound recommendation.

This section has provided a framework for districts to consider as they include strategic planning in their repertoire of organizational strategies to be successful in a nonrational world. The actual model used will vary across districts. But the essence of strategic planning should remain the same: a way of thinking that incorporates data from the external environment with information from the world of the organization—all of this meshed with the culture of the organization to produce recommendations that are economically justifiable, politically attainable, and, last but not least, educationally in the best interests of children.

# 7

# Empowerment

_____

_____

_____

_____

_____

_____

## INTRODUCTION

To review points made in Chapters 2 and 3, power, in its most positive and dynamic sense, is the ability to mobilize the energy within a school district to get things done. As an organizational strategy, empowerment (the process of awarding power) can breathe life and renewal into the organization.

The nonrational view of organizations holds in high esteem three assumptions about empowerment that contribute to the "renewal" orientation. First, empowerment is seen as an expanding entity within the school district. Anyone and any department can have access to the necessary power available. A second assumption is that the acquisition of support (e.g., endorsement by the boss), information (e.g., technical data), and resources (e.g., human services) is the basis by which people and organizational units become empowered. The third assumption states that empowering people in the organization to influence decisions directly affecting them leads to more effective operation of the school district. However, this last assumption does not equate to total delegation or abdication of responsibility. Key organizational decisions maintain their locus of power at the top of the organization.

With these assumptions as guidelines, let's look at how empowerment is manifested at three different locations in the school district: the formal organizational structure, ad hoc problem-solving teams, and individual members of the organization.

## DECENTRALIZED DECISION-MAKING STRUCTURE

As mentioned in Chapter 3, important research on implementation of district projects, as well as the school effectiveness literature, lands solidly on the conclusion that decisions should be made as close to the point of delivery as possible. Implementation is most successful when those affected by a decision have an influence on the decision. The question becomes, What kind of organizational strategy will empower the various units to most effectively achieve district and local school goals? The answer is, Practice the principle of delegation. Actually, this answer calls for some qualification. Delegation is not appropriate when it comes to such areas as school board policymaking, direction expected from the superintendent's office, and decisions necessary to provide consistency and coordination across the district (e.g., bus transportation, major equipment purchases). On the other hand, certain areas of decision making legitimately call for delegation. For example, at the school level, principals and staff should have a major influence in decisions involving curriculum development, teaching strategies, school personnel, and school budgets. This means the central office will have to give up some control in certain areas. But if the data spell out that delegation for decisions such as those just mentioned leads to more effective organizational decisions, justification for clinging to centralized power becomes tenuous at best.

The actual organizational structure for achieving decentralization can take various shapes, depending on the history and culture of the school district. Typically what happens, however, in a decentralized model is that the organizational structure reflects lines of decision making consistent with spheres of responsibility. For example, district instructional decisions are handled at a level within the organizational chart where the central office instructional managers are located. This may mean that the superintendent, while maintaining the right of final decision making, empowers the assistant superintendent of instruction and subordinates with this area of decision making. Decisions affecting schools include the principals in the problem-solving process. Likewise, principals and teachers are empowered to make decisions about teaching and learning that directly affect their student population, unless such a decision is a districtwide policy matter. Delegating district policy amounts to abdication of responsibility by those empowered to deal with districtwide policy issues (e.g., the school board and superintendent of schools).

When all is said and done, the principle of delegation translates into concrete organizational structures conveying the belief that empowerment of organizational units throughout the school district is the most effective organizational strategy for making things happen. The following illustration highlights the principle of delegation.

## SUN VALLEY SCHOOL DISTRICT STUDY

When Mario Sanchez was promoted to superintendent of schools of the Sun Valley School District, he brought with him a long-standing concern that the district's organizational structure was not compatible with the district's guiding beliefs about empowerment. As currently organized, the superintendent's management team consisted of the superintendent, assistant superintendent for instruction, assistant superintendent for business, personnel director, and the director of community relations. Within the instructional services division, the assistant superintendent for instruction chaired a cabinet composed of the director of elementary education, director of secondary education, and coordinators for language arts, math, social studies, and science. Instructional issues of districtwide significance were discussed at the instructional cabinet level, then submitted to the superintendent's management team for final approval.

In his previous role as assistant superintendent, Sanchez served on both the instructional cabinet and the superintendent's management team. He observed that on numerous occasions recommendations reached by the instructional cabinet were modified, sometimes drastically, by the superintendent's management team. Principals, in particular, were troubled by the fact that non-instructional administrators had a major voice on the superintendent's management team regarding instructional issues. Sanchez could recall several instances where the non-instructional team members, while well intended, influenced instructional decisions without adequate data or expertise in the area. Sun Valley principals would be quick to concur with this. In effect, the senior-level instructional administrators were not empowered to get things done within the instructional services division. They had to defer power to the superintendent's management team.

In one of his first actions as superintendent, Sanchez submitted a proposal to the board of education delegating the instructional decision making to the instructional cabinet, with final review by the superintendent. Districtwide policy issues, however, remained within the purview of the superintendent's management team. This new organizational strategy, coupled with the district's guiding belief regarding empowerment, expanded organizational power by (1) freeing the superintendent's management team to spend its power points on items having an impact on the total scope of the district, and (2) allowing the instructional cabinet to assume more direct responsibility for districtwide instructional decisions.

Another effective organizational strategy is to empower local schools with decisions affecting teaching and learning within their sphere of responsibility. This form of empowerment wears several labels: school-based management, school-based budgeting, and school governance. By whatever name, the principle is the same: give the schools sufficient information, resources, and support to mobilize energy at the school level. The case study below describes the organizational strategy of empowerment at the school level.

## EDGERTON SCHOOL DISTRICT STUDY

The Edgerton School District has professed the guiding belief of decentralized decision making in the areas of curriculum, instruction, and personnel for almost a dozen years. Their track record shows they made strides along these lines, with one exception. In practice, the school budgeting process prevented the latitude necessary for making instructional decisions in the best interest of the individual school and community. In other words, daily behavior related to budgeting did not match the guiding belief of decentralization. For example, school budgets were developed along five separate categories:

1. teacher allocations,
2. aide allocations,
3. per pupil improvement funds,
4. program improvement funds, and
5. capital and maintenance funds.

The Edgerton District specified the number of teachers, by subject area, for each school. For example, all elementary schools were assigned 1 librarian, middle schools were assigned 1.5 librarians, and each high school received 3 librarians. After a few years of using this system, principals began complaining about a lack of flexibility in the budgeting process. They felt that more discretion should be allowed in the use of resources to reflect the needs of the individual school. The principals also pointed out that the rather restrictive process currently in place (the daily behavior) did not coincide with the guiding belief of locating decisions as close to the action as possible.

The superintendent of the Edgerton District listened carefully to the principals' pleas and decided to implement school-based budgeting on a pilot basis. Schools participating in the project were empowered to use their various sources of funds in a flexible manner. For example, a typical middle school budget in Edgerton resembled the sample budget in Figure 7.1.

**Fig. 7.1. Sample Middle School Budget**

A.  Teacher allocations __38__  ×  __$30,000__   =               $1,140,000
                                  (average teacher
                                  salary plus
                                  fringes)

        includes 33.5 teachers
                 2.0 counselors
                 1.0 reading teacher
                 1.5 librarians

B.  Aide allocations __2.0__  ×  __$5,500__    =                  11,000

C.  Per pupil formula funds __$85__  ×  __538__   =                45,730
                            rate      enrollment

D.  Program improvement funds                                      3,700

E.  Capital and maintenance                                        7,000
                              Total school budget             $1,207,430

The principal was expected to allocate funds according to the amounts established for each category. In contrast, the middle schools participating in the school-based budgeting pilot project had a different set of ground rules. The principal and staff were empowered to use the $1,207,430 budget in a manner that responded to the individual needs of the school. In other words, staff members were not required to use the money exactly as listed in each category; they had flexibility, for instance, to decide that they needed two fewer teachers, more aide time, and more program improvement funds.

Although the pilot project in the Edgerton School District empowered schools with more control over decisions affecting their school, this did not equate to total autonomy. The superintendent understood that, ultimately, he assumed responsibility for the educational program in the district. Therefore, the school-based budgeting process was subject to review and final action by the superintendent with each school having to justify its recommendations through a budget presentation to the superintendent.

After two years of experimenting with school-based budgeting, the Edgerton District became convinced that this organizational strategy resulted in better decisions about teaching and learning at the school level than a centralized model could provide. Therefore, Edgerton elected to expand school-based budgeting throughout the district.

## EMPOWERMENT THROUGH PROBLEM-SOLVING TEAMS[1]

To be effective in this era of change and uncertainty, a school district requires two types of organizational structures. Every school district needs a formal management structure with specified tasks and lines of authority for carrying out the routine business of the day. Every district also needs another structure, one that is not generally shown on the organizational charts. This "other structure" consists of flexible, ad hoc problem-solving teams—vehicles for figuring out how to do what the organization doesn't yet know.

But "team" doesn't mean just any team. Consistent with the assumptions of integrative systems outlined in Chapter 1 and reinforced in the chapter on strategic planning, organizations need flexible structures that combine ideas from unconnected sources, view problems as "wholes" related to the overall mission of the district, enable multiple perspectives to be taken into consideration, and have the power tools to carry out the assignment. In practice, these structures take the form of participative teams, composed of staff across various departments and assembled on an ad hoc basis to resolve issues that have districtwide implications.

Before moving to a more in-depth analysis of empowerment through participative teams, we should point out that the team approach isn't always the most effective strategy. Under the following conditions, employees don't want or need to be involved:

• when one individual has greater expertise on the subject than others in the school district;

• when the solution has already been determined, so that forming a participative team to "create" a solution would be a waste of organizational energy;

• when an individual has the issue as part of his or her regular assignment;

---

[1] The balance of this chapter draws heavily on two important books by Rosabeth Kanter: *The Change Masters* (1983) and *Men and Women of the Corporation* (1977). Kanter's research provides provocative insights into how organizations work. Although the research is based on private sector data, we feel it has major implications for school districts.

● when no one really cares much about the issue, including instances where the issue is trivial, as well as situations where the problem is so broad it has no meaning to the individual; and
 ● when time dictates a quick decision.

Having acknowledged instances where participative teams would be counterproductive, the organizational strategy of forming integrative teams has proved extremely effective when an organization needs to:

● pool sources of expertise and experience from several departments to solve districtwide issues;
 ● allow those who have knowledge of the issue to get involved;
 ● build organizational ownership on a controversial issue;
 ● balance or confront vested interests;
 ● bring multiple perspectives across departments to a school district issue; and
 ● develop and educate employees through their participation.

Even when the situation clearly warrants the team method, unbridled participation can be disastrous. To effectively use participative teams as an organizational strategy, several dilemmas need to be managed.

## Dilemma of Getting Started

Imposing participation seems like a contradiction of terms. But how does a school district get the ball rolling when it comes to forming teams? If employees are directed to "volunteer" for a project, they likely will be reluctant participants. Also treating participation as a privilege doesn't prove convincing to veteran staff members who realize the time and commitment involved in most committee assignments. To be most effective in gaining participation at the outset of a project, district leadership must clearly describe the purposes of the project, state how the organization will benefit, and indicate the expertise needed to get the job done. As employees who feel a commitment to help the organization perceive they have something substantive to contribute toward the issue at hand, they will more likely consider devoting time to the team.

## Dilemma of Structure and Management

Problem-solving teams face the curse of too much freedom. Vague, muddled, contradictory messages about purpose, timeline, and available power lead to immobilization. The committee then wastes valuable time clarifying purpose, debating timeline, and wondering if they have the clout to make things happen. In contrast, when an ad hoc team has a clearly defined structure specifying the limits, timeline, political realities, and committee charge, they can channel their energy toward the issue, without spending precious time wondering what they're supposed to do and how they're going to do it.

A related dilemma is one of leadership. Senior officials must strike a balance between giving up total control of the group and holding too tightly to the reins. Delegation, in its optimal sense, means initially setting the parameters, then staying involved through coordinating resources, reviewing progress reports, and being available to meet with teams at critical junctures. Specified relationships between senior management responsible for convening the team and the team itself signal to members that top management does care about and value the work put forth by the team.

## Dilemma of Teamwork

For most members of a team, participative decision making means just that: involvement and influence regarding the issues facing the team. Kanter (1983) observed four types of inequalities that can create an unhealthy balance between team members' participation.

*Imposition of the hierarchy.* For problem-solving teams to be effective in an integrative environment, they need to be drawn from across departments and organizational levels. However, if the higher level administrators assume a privileged position in the group, what was a strength can quickly become a weakness. By reproducing the organization chart within the team, lower status people in the district assume lower status roles in the problem-solving team. To avoid this imposition of the formal hierarchy, senior officials forming the team plus the higher level members on the team must demonstrate that for the purposes of the team assignment, all members enter the team arrangements at an equal level.

*Knowledge gap.* Another entry level dilemma is presence of a knowledge gap in the teams. Unless the gap is minimized or eliminated, the poorly informed compete with the highly informed (who, on most policy issues, usually are the higher level administrators) as they struggle to make cooperative decisions. In actuality, the less knowledgeable team members lose credibility in a hurry, consequently losing power to influence decisions. This condition undermines the productivity of the team and the legitimacy of the process. One way to close the knowledge gap is to make the necessary information, resources, and support equally available to all team members. In addition, when the team is formed, all participants should be given a thorough briefing regarding whatever background information is necessary to operate successfully in the group.

*Personal resource gap.* Inevitably, people bring to the team setting an unequal distribution of personal characteristics and skills. A combination of verbal skills, the ability to conceptualize issues within the broader context of values, issues and overall direction of the school district, plus previous experience in cross-departmental problem-solving teams enhances the power of these individuals. A major responsibility of group leadership under these conditions is to first recognize these differences when they occur, control the "air time" of the more verbal members of the group, and try to show that the immediate problems of the group aren't highly dependent on what group members have contributed in their previous experience on problem-solving teams. The group leader should also encourage those with a "personal resource gap deficiency" to become more verbal and become familiar with the broader context of district operations.

*Internal politics of teams.* A school district's guiding belief about the importance of teamwork gets shoved to the background if, in real life, teams bring to the group self-serving interests and a segmentalist view of organizational decision making. Politics become thickest when team members feel they must compete to garner resources for themselves or their department and when they believe their major role on the team is to represent their departmental or school interests. Conversely, cooperation can be enhanced if the participants serve as individuals, not as messengers for a constituency. This can be encouraged by clarifying the district belief that "we believe in an integrated approach to problem solving. We're all in this business together, working cooperatively, not competitively, to achieve school district goals."

Another source of political tension within groups is the convening of people who represent factions that have a history of hostility and mistrust. Bringing these tensions to the team table likely will lead to even more hostility and eventually to diminished group productivity. A successful strategy used in labor management groups is to lay a careful groundwork consisting of improved communication channels, demonstrations of good faith efforts on mutually important issues, and resolution of nuisance issues before the team is called together. Suppose, for instance, a school district administration wants to form a joint committee of teacher union representatives and senior school district officials to develop ways to give teachers more recognition. Assuming such a cooperative venture has never before been proposed, the superintendent probably will need to meet quietly with union leaders in advance to build a trust level, establish informal communication between the two groups, and head off as many issues as possible before the group is convened.

If, for example, the union is wary that decisions made by the committee will be seen as preempting the official union decision-making process, the superintendent and union president could strike an agreement to refer all decisions that have possible teacher contract implications to the union bureaucracy for approval. By resolving this issue ahead of time, the union-administration committee can avoid these politics in committee.

## Dilemma of Winding Down

Once team members overcome barriers to success, they may find that the taste of success is one worth sustaining. Relinquishing power isn't easy, and the amount of power accruing to a well-oiled team is formidable. Often these teams stand ready to expand their original charge or look for completely new assignments to the point of lobbying for standing committee status. A related dilemma is development of primary allegiance to the team rather than to their original constituency. This allegiance makes it even more difficult to wind down. Therefore, careful planning is necessary to orchestrate the life and death of the teams, and ground rules must be established that spell out the conditions signaling their demise.

# GUIDELINES FOR PARTICIPATIVE DECISION MAKING

Participation is not *the answer* to solving all organizational problems. It is, however, a viable strategy that empowers people across the school district to pool their information, resources, and support networks in an effort to tackle tough problems as they emerge in the district. As this section has illustrated, even when teamwork seems the most logical approach to school district problem solving, making this process work effectively is not an easy matter. To be effective, participative decision-making teams should operate within the following guidelines:

- assignment of meaningful, manageable tasks with clear boundaries;
- a carefully delineated time frame and set of reporting relationships;
- a mechanism for involving all of those parties with a stake in the issue;
- a mechanism for providing visibility, reward, and recognition for team efforts; and
- clearly understood processes for the formation and dissolving of groups, along with an understanding of how their work will be used after the life of the team.

For a school district to be successful in the use of participative decision-making teams, the district must invest a lot of energy in attending to the conceptual and practical details of making them function effectively. However, the end product is worth it: a process for energizing the grass roots and empowering them in an integrative way to strengthen the organization.

## POWER THROUGH PEOPLE

Traditionally, power has been associated with titles and placement on the organizational chart. But real empowerment, the ability to get things done, comes from access to the power tools of support, information, and resources. As school districts seek to expand access to power within the organization, they realize that a critical organizational strategy is to empower individuals. This can occur in two ways, through selected activities and through the building of alliances.

### Empowerment Through Selected Activities

Individual employees usually don't accumulate power points by performing their assignment in a routine manner. Even doing an excellent job of what is expected doesn't enhance a person's status in the organization. According to Kanter (1977), only selected types of job activities increase the power of persons within the organization. Specifically, activities contributing to empowerment should meet three criteria: (1) they are extraordinary, (2) they are visible, and (3) they are relevant to pressing organizational problems.

*Extraordinary activities.* If the school district routinizes all assignments by reducing opportunities for creativity, risk taking, and experimentation, the district diminishes any hopes for people to perform in extraordinary fashion. In contrast, enterprising school districts can actually create opportunities for extraordinary activities in several ways. First, districts can construct new, exciting positions with access to necessary power tools. Employees who are the rising stars could be encouraged to assume these positions, thereby enhancing their personal power, as well as contributing strength to the organization. A second way to engage in extraordinary activities is to innovate. Employees who are willing to take risks by staking claim to innovative projects can accumulate resources, information, and support for the subsequent activities. If successful in their venture, employees can count on added empowerment within the organization.

*Visibility.* Invisible assignments are those which are part of the standard operating procedures of the district. Just being a principal doesn't automatically create visibility. For activities to enhance power, they have to attract the attention of others in the school district. For example, jobs that bridge more than one department tend to be more conspicuous (e.g., the coordinator of nursing services who works directly with the department of pupil services and the curriculum department). Similarly, having contact on a regular basis with special education staff as well as regular education staff or having the opportunity to work in more than one school heightens visibility.

Another way to be noticed is through participation on key committees. In general, serving on a school reading committee isn't enough. However, working on a joint teacher-administrator committee reviewing the teacher evaluation system likely will lead to districtwide exposure. Also, being selected to participate on a citizen-school district task force charged with developing recommendations for desegregation probably will be an attention-getter.

A third source of visibility is frequent job mobility. This isn't job-hopping every year or two. But a change every three or four years gives the employee multiple perspectives on the organization and gives him or her more exposure across the district. As people move around, they have the opportunity to strengthen their repertoire of power tools. They also can strengthen the network of people who can help them mobilize resources in the district. This breadth of knowledge about the district and increased contact through the organization especially come in handy when individuals are seeking promotion in the organization.

*Relevancy.* Even extraordinary and visible activities won't necessarily lead to individual empowerment without the third ingredient—relevance, which is defined as whether or not the activities are associated with pressing school district issues. As an illustration, assume a school principal decided to press for educational reform by developing a continuous progress program in the school. The purpose of such a program is to do away with grade levels and to allow students to learn at a pace and level appropriate for them. The project may be considered extraordinary and highly visible. But assume also that the school board, applying the rational model, is in the middle of trying to standardize its curriculum across all schools. Clearly the continuous progress program fails the relevance test. In fact, it proves contrary to the districtwide issue of standardizing curriculum. Conclusion: no added empowerment within the organization for the principal. On the other hand, imagine a principal who responds to the school board's effort to decentralize curriculum decision making by volunteering to be one of three schools in the district to try school-based budgeting. Assuming the project is highly successful, with teachers expressing strong satisfaction because they have more influence over local curriculum matters, then power will accrue to the principal because all three criteria are met: the project was extraordinary, highly visible, and relevant to district issues.

## Empowerment Through Alliances

A sometimes overlooked basis for individual empowerment in a school district comes from colleagues working at various levels in the hierarchy. In this section we describe how empowerment results from three sets of connections: senior-level administrators, peers, and subordinates.

*Sponsors.* Because of their position and ready access to power, the leadership of an organization has the clout to empower those at lower rungs on the organizational ladder. Referred to as sponsors, these senior-level administrators play four important functions in the empowerment process. First, they assume responsibility for ensuring that appropriate introductions are made to key administrators in the organizational hierarchy. Second, sponsors can defend an individual when he or she is the center of controversy during closed-door management meetings. Or, on the positive side, sponsors can recommend an individual for promising assignments, which will further empower the employee. Third, sponsors can cut red tape, bypassing the usual chain of command. By extending a "drop by anytime" invitation to selected individuals, sponsors can dispense information and short-cut the formal communication structure via these informal relationships. The fourth function of sponsors is to provide powerful backing at strategic times. For employees located in middle and lower slots on the organizational chart, a big chunk of empowerment comes from the credits they've earned through access to resources in the form of backing by influential administrators. One note of caution, however: the wider the organizational distance between sponsor and the person sponsored, the more tenuous the empowerment relationship. Individuals should not place all their chips on the backing of a single sponsor.

*Peers.* In research conducted within the corporate sector, peer acceptance was identified as a prerequisite to building a power base. As individuals move through the ranks, they find that their track record for working with peers becomes critical in future situations where power tools are needed. For instance, if an entry level administrator developed a reputation for sharing information and sharing success with peers, this reputation can be a powerful lever (even in the form of accumulated chips) as the individual moves up the organizational ladder. Suppose, for instance, a middle school principal in the Fort Sioux School District applies for the position of director of secondary education. Members of the selection committee who are peers of the candidate recall and speak favorably of instances where the candidate went to extra lengths to work cooperatively with colleagues and assumed a major leadership role among middle school principals as they revised their curriculum. Such a solid reputation among peers proved to be the swing factor in choosing the middle school principal for the director position.

*Subordinates.* Empowerment doesn't always flow from the top down. Senior administrators can enhance their own power by building alliances with subordinates, particularly the rising stars. In its most extreme and selfish case, sustaining these alliances becomes important because the subordinate could suddenly become the boss. More often, though, senior administrators must count on those lower on the organizational chart to implement policies and programs that the board of education and top administration develop. In addition, high level administrators acquire extra credibility and concomitant empowerment points when they can take credit for rising stars under their tutelage.

## Hollow Power: Accountability Without Clout

So far, the discussion has highlighted the ingredients for individual empowerment, ways in which employees can build a power base with the help of superordinates, peers, and subordinates. The flip side of this discussion centers on those who have power officially vested in their position but end up powerless in a practical sense.

One of the worst situations for managers is when their position holds them accountable for certain results but they lack the ability and credibility to fulfill the expectations of their position. Consider, for example, a director of elementary education who supervises all elementary principals in a school district. If the director can't run effective meetings, can't satisfactorily resolve disputes among the principals, and doesn't understand the district budgeting process, it won't take long for the principals to turn to someone else (e.g., the superintendent) for help. When this happens, certain behavior patterns can be anticipated. First, the director of elementary education will boss whomever he or she can. The irony of this behavior is that the director (who is practically powerless) may attempt to be more controlling than ever. Without the usual empowerment tools available, this administrator likely will resort to the levers of reward and punishment. Rewards take the form of bending rules, and punishment occurs through enforcing the rules. When these power tactics result in resistance and anger by elementary principals, the director may resort to more controlling behavior.

A second behavior pattern of powerless leaders is a low-risk, play-it-safe attitude. Making sure that everything is done right is the only response for those who lack sufficient empowerment, and they demand this kind of ritualistic conformity from subordinates. In response to organizational powerlessness, these managers guard their own territory jealously. They "wall off" their turf and protect against any intrusion from outside their division. They also discourage those within the division from going beyond the division boundaries for resources to get the job done. This behavior results in the segmentalist approach to organizational life that we have identified as contributing to organizational ineffectiveness.

## CONCLUSION

The above discussion graphically illustrates the importance of empowerment in order to make things happen within a school district. Those who secure empowerment points beyond their official boundaries establish increased credibility, which serves as a basis for more power. As Kanter put it (1977):

The powerful are not only given material and symbolic advantages but they are also provided with circumstances that can make them more effective mobilizers of other people. Thus they can accomplish and, through their accomplishments, generate more power. As this builds, they can build alliances, with other people as colleagues rather than threats, and through their alliances generate more power (p. 196).

In contrast, the powerless are caught in a downward spiral. The controlling behavior of powerless leaders elicits further resistance to power, provoking more rule-minded attempts at power, leading to a segmental orientation with no rewards for risk taking, change, and ultimately growth.

In today's changing environment, school districts can't afford a segmental orientation. They need leadership with a vision of how to integrate the concepts of the nonrational model with flexible organizational strategies designed to anticipate changing conditions in order to most effectively carry out the mission of the district. The leadership characteristics for such a challenging assignment are the subject of Chapter 8.

# 8

# Leadership in a Nonrational World

## INTRODUCTION

It is appropriate to move immediately from a discussion of empowerment into a discussion of leadership, since empowering others is one of the most important things an effective leader can do. In one sense, the effective leader serves as a power source for the organization. However, rather than doling out portions of a fixed entity to fortunate others, the effective leader in the nonrational organization generates power. Under the leader's successful efforts at empowerment, power grows as an entity in the organization.

## A FRAMEWORK FOR LEADERSHIP

It should be apparent that a great deal is called for from a leader in the circumstances of rapid change and conflict we have described. Such a person must grasp the organizational concepts discussed so far and be able to implement the strategies we have developed. All the excellence literature, both that about schools and the private sector as well, converges on the importance of effective leaders.

At the outset, we need to construct a framework that will underscore the importance of the nonrational world's context for leadership. This framework is built on the material in the preceding chapters. This context for leadership is as important as the leadership qualities we are about to discuss. Otherwise, there is a danger that the qualities we develop will lose any meaning except for their conventional denotations, which have the character of leadership literature clichés. For example, it is useless to suggest that a leader needs to have vision, unless that quality is anchored in the context of a nonrational view of organizations. If vision is not informed by knowledge of that context, in our judgment it may become delusion.

With this caveat, then, the leader in a nonrational world must be capable of assuming responsibility for the sequence of activities outlined in Figure 8.1. Each of these activities is developed in the following sections.

**Fig. 8.1. Leadership in a Nonrational World**

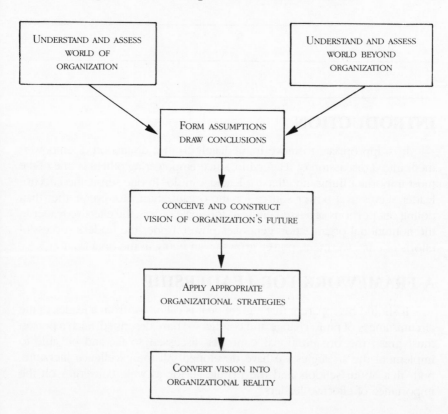

## Understanding and Assessing the World Within and Beyond the Organization

The leader must know how organizations really operate, and not rely solely on traditional views of how they should operate. The leader must understand both the rational and nonrational models for thinking about organizations and reality.

Knowing the world within the organization means knowing the culture and knowing how to work with it. Persuasiveness, teaching ability, and the ability to manage symbols are important skills. Rosabeth Kanter (1983) describes skill "in persuading others to invest information, support, and resources in new initiatives..." as a "power skill" (pp. 35–36). We have previously mentioned her definition of those three commodities as tools for empowerment of others. Naturally, the effective leader will be skillful in convincing people in the organization to invest their resources in promising initiatives, and by doing so will increase the power and cohesiveness of the organizational culture.

The leader also influences the culture of the school district by serving in the role of teacher. The effective leader continuously teaches the vision, values, mission, goals, and objectives of the organization to others. In this context, leadership means assuming responsibility for creating a flow of purposeful and unifying images throughout the organizational culture.

As an adjunct to teaching and persuasion, as well as to establishing the proper organizational culture to support innovation, a leader must know the importance of symbols and have skill at using them. For example, symbol management includes: consistently reinforcing the values most important to the organization, distributing reward and praise to those who perform well, attending events that have symbolic importance to the district, and repeatedly emphasizing those accomplishments that demonstrate constancy in purpose within the organization. Through leader behavior in these and other areas, images are created that come to characterize the organization.

The nonrational leader must have a solid understanding and knowledge of those demographic and cultural trends outlined in Chapter 1. These trends represent an important aspect of the world beyond the organization—the external environment. Further, a leader needs a personal strategy for environmental scanning, in order to stay abreast of change in the external environment. This is not a task that can be done once, then forgotten. The monitoring and interpreting of events is something the nonrational leader does continuously and systematically. This skill is referred to as versatility by some writers, and is paired with focus (Hickman and Silva 1984, pp. 199–200). Focus requires concentration on details—a few at a time. Versatility requires the opposite—"the capacity to embrace and participate in an ever-changing world" (Hickman and Silva 1984, p. 177). Versatility helps to anticipate change, focus to implement it.

## Forming Assumptions and Drawing Conclusions

Having successfully achieved a solid understanding of the world within and beyond the school district, the leader must use these data to form assumptions and conclusions about the organization and the external environment in which the organization is operating. For instance, the five "new" assumptions listed in Chapter 1 might be likely ones. This all merges into a unified view of the organizational gestalt, and allows the leader to begin to see a direction and future for the organization. Then the nonrational leader must take perhaps the most difficult step:

## Conceiving of and Constructing a Vision of the Organization's Future

Vision is a mental journey from the known to the unknown (Hickman and Silva 1984, p. 151). The leader creates a future from a montage of facts, hopes, dreams, and forecasts. Vision is the product of exercising many skills in a holistic way to create a mental picture of what the future could and should look like. It is not undisciplined daydreaming; it is more than a short intuitive flash. This developing vision has four dimensions.

*Foresight.* Looking into the future, the leader is able to sense not only what will happen, but on what time schedule, to anticipate those items that need short-, medium-, and long-range planning. The leader develops a special feel for time, including a sense of the rates of change and the time required to plan and respond.

*Hindsight.* At the same time, the leader looks backward. The developing vision cannot violate the cultural norms of the organization. The history of the organization—its past trials, heroes, and symbols—is critical in building the future. The external environment's history in regard to the organization and its past is also crucial. The nonrational leader finds ways to learn about this past, and how to interpret it.

A note of caution is needed here. Typically, unexamined individual and collective visions of the past tend to err—usually in the direction of a more positive interpretation than the actual reality would warrant. The tendency is to look back on the past as a kind of "golden age" or "Camelot," perhaps stemming from a natural human ability to suppress bad experience. As an effective use of hindsight, the nonrational leader may have the unpleasant task of correcting such unexamined visions of the past for the benefit of the rest of the organization.

*Depth perception.* The nonrational leader is able to see the big picture, to see how all the parts work together as a total system. The leader also is capable of holding different points of view so that multiple possibilities can be seen. For instance, the nonrational educational leader can see things from the instructional side and from the business side, from the view of the personnel director, from the view of the principals, from the union leaders and the rank and file. Depth perception extends beyond knowing the traditional wisdom about how various groups see the world. Leadership means understanding what life looks and feels like for these people in this particular organization. Understanding and assessing the organizational culture is invaluable in developing depth perception.

*Peripheral vision.* We have already stated the need for scanning beyond the organization; the nonrational leader needs to know what's going on "out there," and needs a systematic way of staying informed. It should be stressed here that the leader doesn't seek just a random collection of facts about the periphery of the organization. In fact, in each of these four directional metaphors for vision, the emphasis is on synthesizing what is known into a cohesive picture that will contribute to the leader's ultimate vision for the organization.

In summary, the visionary leader does more than dream in a stream of consciousness fashion. Each of the dimensions just described combines to create vision with a focus. Next, the leader is ready to start making the vision a reality.

The effective leader will seek the most powerful way to present this vision to the rest of the organization. Communication skills, particularly creative ones, are important at this point. Fluency in creating effective analogies, metaphors, and symbols is essential. Like the late Ray Kroc of McDonald's fame, the leader must help others see "beauty in a burger." A recent example that came to our attention may help.

The leader and staff of a gifted and talented program housed as a separate school in its own building had been hoping that the district's reorganization plan would move them to a new site. The program had experienced a number of problems, and many negative feelings were associated with their current physical plant. However, district action, while removing the source of some key instructional problems, left the program at its current site. The leader told us that she and her staff felt as if they had been placed in a building that was then wrapped tightly with Saran Wrap. She was reminded, however, that some key problems were eliminated. She agreed, and then, in order to change this suffocating vision of the future, the leader decided to create a new image and share it with the staff. She decided to envision the building as wrapped in soap bubbles, in order to present to her staff a feeling of new freedom and opportunity. She and the staff then decided to start the next school year by having everyone, including the students, write their frustrations on helium balloons and release these as a first-day activity. This image has started the staff on a number of other innovative ideas for the coming year. It serves as an example to show how selection and communication of images can transform what is essentially the same situation from a problem to an opportunity.

## Applying Appropriate Organizational Strategies

In earlier chapters, we discussed two major organizational strategies: strategic planning and empowerment. The effective nonrational leader has major responsibilities and competencies in these two areas.

*Strategic planning.* This organizational strategy flows from three assumptions:

1. The nonrational model accurately describes the real world.

2. We live in a dynamic world of rapid change; this is not just a temporary condition until we get a rational handle on things.

3. The external world is inextricably bound into our planning efforts.

With these assumptions in place, leadership skills become critical in the areas of scanning, monitoring, and interpreting the environment and the organization. Successful leaders need the skill to focus simultaneously on the past, present, and future, combining the skills of historian and futurist. With the rapid pace of change, a leader will find timelines for implementation evaporating unless he or she has a good sense of the flow and meaning of events in the nonrational world.

Another quality that is valuable in strategic planning is patience. Strangely, perhaps, patience is a skill related to vision, and an enabling skill that assists other skills to be effective. As Hickman and Silva put it (1984, p. 223), "If you have developed a thoughtful strategy and have fostered the kind of culture you need to implement it successfully, you must be patient to see your vision through to its conclusion. Otherwise, you probably lack faith in your vision." While we will not discuss "faith" as an attribute of leadership, the reader could contemplate its place in the scheme of things. Impatience for quick fixes and bottom line returns, coupled with a lack of faith, has probably destroyed many good corporate visions.

*Empowerment.* Empowerment occurs when more people and units in the organization gain access to support, information, and resources. Previously, we argued that people could be empowered at three levels in the organization: the formal structure, ad hoc teams, and individual members of the organization. The effective nonrational leader needs to have skill in working with each of these levels.

The leader sees units of the organization as interdependent and sets up structures that create an integrated system, with cross-cutting relationships and decentralized decision making. When decision making is decentralized, the leader needs skill in persuading others to invest their efforts in the ideas of entrepreneurs and creative subunits. The leader needs to be especially skilled in bridging the gaps between interest groups.

The leader also must have skill in setting up ad hoc problem-solving teams. These teams are formed in such a way that they combine ideas from unconnected sources, view problems as wholes, take multiple perspectives on issues, and have the power tools to carry out the assignment. In providing the power tools, the leader again has to be effective in persuading others to invest time, information, and resources in teamwork. The effective leader also needs to have skills in managing the problems and dilemmas that occur with the use of teams. Some major skills that help here are sensitivity, patience, appraisal skill, versatility, and teaching ability. These skills will also have been used in creating the organizational structures, and they will be vital in the third level of empowerment.

The third level is empowering people. Here, the leader empowers people by assigning extraordinary activities, by rewarding star performers, and by forming empowering alliances. Making the proper choices here requires the nonrational leader to exhibit analytical skills, intuitional skills, and interpersonal skills.

## Converting Vision into Organizational Reality

The logical conclusion from following the above steps over time will be to convert the vision the leader had for the organization into reality. Communication skills mentioned earlier are particularly critical in this conversion process. The organization should not be configured in a way that reflects the vision. The organizational reality will reflect not only an understanding of the organization on the part of the leader but also an understanding of the context for organization. The culture of the organization will be known to the leader; its symbols, rituals, and guiding beliefs will be known to all. The organization will behave in ways consistent with its beliefs. Ultimately, the existence of a healthy organizational culture will be the litmus test of whether a proper vision has been successfully converted to organizational reality.

# LEADERSHIP SKILLS

Throughout the previous section, we referred to a variety of leadership skills, abilities, and qualities that are dependent on the context in which they are being exercised. We do acknowledge that a repertoire of skills is important. It might now seem appropriate to proceed with a list of skills, which we then would formally define and discuss. However, to create a list and discuss each skill in turn has a pitfall. Providing such a list implies the skills are discrete and logically leads one to a skill development approach to leadership. While we would agree that work on discrete skill development could be incidentally helpful to the prospective leader, our basic position is that good leadership comes from thinking about organizations in certain ways, and then taking appropriate action based on that thought. In other words, the leader needs the nonrational model and its strategies to shape his or her thought and action. The skills, abilities and qualities must operate in concert to create that thought and action—rarely are they separately or serially exercised.

Having made a pitch to avoid separation, we want to violate our own rule. There *is* one quality, above all others, that serves as a center to hold things together in a nonrational world. It is the one characteristic that is absolutely essential to leadership, binding all skills into an effective whole. It is integrity.

# THE FUNDAMENTAL NATURE OF INTEGRITY

The word "integrity" comes from a Latin root that means "whole" or "entire." The word itself means that something is sound; in an unimpaired and uncompromised condition. It also can mean adherence to a code of values, be they moral or artistic. When applied to people, it carries a sense of incorruptibility and wholeness. People who have integrity have a strong center or core of values and skills that hold things together. The concept we discuss comprises all the above elements.

Some 1,500 managers and executives were asked to identify and rank qualities most admired in subordinates, colleagues, and superiors. Integrity was the highest rated quality for all three groups. For superiors, it even ranked ahead of the quality of leadership. A related concept, honesty, also ranks high in such surveys, as does responsibility. We argue that it is this "integrity complex" that serves to hold together all the previously discussed dimensions of leadership. In fact, Cunningham (1985, p. 20) cites integrity as a key symbol or hallmark for the quality organization, as well as the leader. Without it, organizational endeavors and leader behavior can deteriorate into ad hoc opportunism.

If integrity, through leader modeling, becomes a guiding belief of the culture, it has great power. A leader who demonstrates such qualities inspires trust in subordinates. The leader will not have to constantly prove the good intent of his or her actions. Further, if integrity is a guiding principle, then the leader can trust subordinates. This in turn opens the door to decentralized decision making, teaming, and empowerment—basics for making the nonrational organization successful.

It could be argued that integrity can't be taught, that it is part of one's character. Perhaps. But we feel integrity can be willed in an individual and created in the organization. It is a matter of personal choice. And so, the principle is under the control of individuals and organizations, which is all that matters. We also feel that conscious application of the other skills, attributes, qualities, and processes of the nonrational leadership model will have the effect of creating many opportunities for integrity to be exercised and thus practiced.

In summary, the integrity of the leader and the organization created by the leader's vision becomes the point of stability for people in the rapidly changing and ambiguous social environment described by the nonrational model. And so, again, without this central anchoring place, attempts to deal with the rapid change of our world through adjustments in the organization will probably be unsuccessful, even if some other aspects of the nonrational model are in place.

# 9

# The Nonrational Model Applied to the School

_____

_____

_____

_____

_____

## INTRODUCTION

Up to now our analysis has dealt primarily with the organization of the school district. While we have occasionally made reference to school buildings or to school principals, we have not applied the nonrational model to the world of the school. We firmly believe, however, that the principles embedded in the book thus far are relevant to the organization of the individual school. In this chapter we illustrate how the nonrational world view can be used to think about schools by discussing two aspects of school organization that are crucial to understanding and promoting school improvement: building culture and principal leadership.

In the discussion that follows we do not simply transfer ideas and terms from the district to the school. In part this is because the two organizational levels are dissimilar enough that substituting "school" for "district" and "principal" for "superintendent" could be misleading. But, it is also due to our belief that the nonrational world view is not a formula to be mechanically applied. Instead, it is a way of thinking about organizations, in this case educational organizations, that is powerful precisely because it more accurately reflects the changing reality of those organizations. While this chapter is not an exhaustive treatment of the nonrational model and school building organization, it does provide guidance as school administrators contemplate professional activities in a nonrational world.

## SCHOOL CULTURE

Within school districts, a special form of subculture is the culture of the school. In fact, school culture has become particularly significant as researchers attempt to uncover the characteristics of effective schools.

For instance, from an effort to understand why some elementary schools are relatively more successful than other schools serving similar populations of students, culture has emerged as the most persuasive explanation (Brookover et al. 1979, Cohen 1983, Hawley et al. 1984, MacKenzie 1983, Purkey and Smith 1983). Schools considered more "satisfying" by teachers and students had different cultures than did schools deemed less satisfying (Goodlad 1984). Middle schools judged as contributing to positive adolescent development were described as having distinct cultures or "personalities" (Lipsitz 1984). The "goodness" ascribed to exemplary high schools by Lightfoot (1983) referred to the schools' overall culture rather than to five or six distinct elements. In the debate over the merits of public versus private schools, the culture of private schools is assumed to be partially responsible for their alleged superiority (e.g., see Coleman et al. 1982). Research into the implementation of innovations has sharpened our understanding of the power of school culture in determining the fate of proposed reforms (see Sarason 1971), and recent discussions of teacher effectiveness have emphasized the influence of aspects of the school culture on classroom climate and instructional techniques (e.g., Lieberman and Miller 1984, Rosenholtz 1985). Finally, though they do not speak directly of school culture, the reforms proposed by Boyer (1983) and Sizer (1984) would alter the organizational structure, normative values, patterns of behavior, and so on, of high schools and result in the development of new institutional cultures at the building level.

In discussing school-level culture, a degree of confusion unfortunately arises from the use of multiple terms. Some researchers favor *ethos* (e.g., Rutter et al. 1979) or *climate* (e.g., Goodlad 1984), while others substitute *moral order* (Cohen 1983) or *learning environment* (Hawley et al. 1984). Still others talk about school social systems and separate culture from social structure (Brookover et al. 1979), and a few attempt to expand the concept of culture by locating it within an ecological perspective (see Anderson 1982).

Admittedly, it is inaccurate to employ these terms interchangeably. However, for our purposes the phenomena all these terms represent can legitimately be included within the concept of culture. Therefore, to reduce confusion we use *culture* here to refer to those aspects of the school that generally reflect or structure the guiding beliefs and daily behavior of staff and students.

A second difficulty in examining school culture arises from the lack of precision with which we can evaluate culture at the building level. Readily available and easily used instruments are not yet widely available to assess the nature of a school's culture. Of those that are reasonably accessible, few appear to be have been submitted to rigorous tests for reliability or validity (Guzzetti 1983). However, at least two instruments (Connecticut State Department of Education's school effectiveness questionnaires; Santa Clara County Office of Education's basic school profile) seem to differentiate among schools and can serve as models for other schools and districts. At a more informal level, however, even the casual visitor can detect variations in the "feel" of a school, variations that we argue are due to the differing cultures of each building. The problem, of course, is how to make something that is palpable and powerful, but difficult to quantify, work for us (Deal and Kennedy 1983).

Before suggesting a framework for assessing building culture, here is a summary of what the present knowledge base tells us about school culture.[1]

• School culture does affect the behavior and achievement of elementary and secondary school students (though the effect of classroom and student variables remains greater).

• School culture does not fall from the sky; it is created and thus can be manipulated by people within the school.

• School cultures are relatively unique; whatever their commonalities (e.g., sense of leadership, clear and shared goals), no two schools will be exactly alike—nor should they be.

• The elements of school cultures interact with each other to produce a whole that is greater than the sum of its parts; while individual aspects of the school culture can affect a child for better or worse, it is the child's encounter with the entire school culture that seems most influential.

• Particularly, but not exclusively, at the secondary level, different groups of students (subpopulations) experience the school's culture differently; simi-

---

[1] See Anderson 1982, Bacharach et al. 1986, Brookover et al. 1979, Cohen 1983, Coleman et al. 1982, Goodlad 1984, Hawley et al. 1984, Lieberman and Miller 1984, Lightfoot 1983, Lipsitz 1984, MacKenzie 1983, Purkey and Smith 1983, Rosenholtz 1985, Rutter et al. 1979, and Sarason 1971.

larly, students' peer cultures and/or community cultures may not be in harmony with the school's.

• To the extent that it provides a focus and clear purpose for the school, culture becomes the cohesion that bonds the school together as it goes about its mission.

• Though we concentrate on its beneficial nature, culture can be counterproductive and an obstacle to educational success; culture can also be oppressive and discriminatory for various subgroups within the school.

• Lasting, fundamental change (e.g., in organizational process or teacher behaviors) requires understanding and, often, altering the school's culture; cultural change is generally a slow process.

## The Characteristics of a Healthy School Culture

With these summary statements in mind, we turn to the components of a school culture that are conducive to teaching and learning. The specific list of components can vary depending on whose research is cited. We think that there is insufficient evidence to permit selecting any one portrait as the best analysis. Moreover, there is a great deal of similarity among the portraits—for example, all include strong leadership (though the potential sources may vary), all emphasize order and discipline (though the conceptions of an orderly environment may vary), and most acknowledge the importance of collaborative work and planning (though the extent to which decision making is democratized may vary).

It could be argued, therefore, that choosing a description of an effective school culture is largely a matter of institutional preference. School improvement then becomes a matter of using the list of research-based characteristics as a tool to assess the school's culture and as a guide in generating a coherent and systematic plan that mobilizes the school's staff to collectively work toward specific goals.

However, different descriptions of effective school cultures reflect somewhat different assumptions about the educational outcomes that are valued or given precedence. For example, some lists emphasize basic skills acquisition (e.g., Brookover et al. 1979, Edmonds 1979) and are not concerned with changing the nature of the school as a workplace for the staff or with reducing alienation by fostering community feeling among staff and students. In that light, the choice of a particular portrait of an effective school culture is important, precisely because it shapes the process and content of the change process. With this influence in mind, we have selected the 13 characteristics presented by Purkey and Smith (1983) that were developed out of a cultural perspective on school change. Implicit in their conceptualization is an orientation toward academic achievement as a valued student outcome and toward staff collaboration and shared decision making as a means of improving the quality of institutional life in schools.

As described by Purkey and Smith (1985, pp. 358–359), the 13 characteristics of a good school culture are as follows.

1. *School site management and democratic decision making.* Staffs of each building are given a considerable amount of responsibility and authority in determining the exact means by which they address the problem of increasing academic performance. This includes giving staffs more authority over curricular and instructional decisions and allocation of building resources.

2. *Leadership.* Though we are suspicious of the "great principal" theory, strong leadership from administrators, teachers, or integrated teams of both is necessary to initiate and maintain the improvement process. Lacking indigenous leadership, outside change facilitators must be provided.

3. *Staff stability.* Frequent transfers are likely to retard, if not prevent, the growth of a coherent and ongoing school personality, especially in early phases of the change process.

4. *Curriculum articulation and organization.* A planned, coordinated curriculum that increases the amount of time students spend studying basic skills and other academic disciplines is likely to be more productive than the broad curriculum common in many schools today. A rich, in-depth curriculum at the secondary level that challenges all students, though not directly suggested by the effective schools literature, may be preferable to the superficial study of many subjects (Sizer 1984).

5. *Staff development.* Schoolwide staff development is ongoing and links the expressed concerns of the staff to the school's specific instructional and organizational needs.

6. *Parental involvement and support.* Though the evidence is mixed in the area of parental involvement in daily school activities, obtaining parental support of school homework, attendance, and discipline policies is likely to influence student performance positively, perhaps by increasing motivation.

7. *Schoolwide recognition of academic success.* Publicly honoring academic achievement (including showing improvement, as well as reaching standards of excellence) and stressing its importance encourage students to adopt similar norms and values.

8. *Maximized learning time.* More of the school day and more of the class period are devoted to active learning activities in academic areas; class periods are free from interruptions and disruptions.

9. *District support.* Fundamental change, building-level management, staff stability, and so on, depend on support from the district office; district

recognition of school staffs' efforts and the provision of necessary resources are necessary to the improvement process.

10. *Collaborative planning and collegial relationships.* Change attempts are more successful when teachers and administrators work together; collegiality breaks down barriers between departments and among teachers and administrators, encourages the kind of intellectual sharing that can lead to consensus, and promotes feelings of unity and commonality among the staff.

11. *Sense of community.* Schools build feelings of community that contribute to reduced alienation and increased performance of students and staff alike.

12. *Clear goals and high expectations commonly shared.* Schools whose staff agree on their goals (e.g., academic achievement) and expectations (e.g., for work and achievement from all students) are more likely to be successful in that they have channeled their energy and efforts toward a mutually agreed upon purpose.

13. *Order and discipline.* The seriousness and purposefulness with which the school approaches its tasks are communicated by the order and discipline it maintains in its building and classrooms; rules are established by mutual agreement, consistently and fairly enforced.

This list is not intended to be a blueprint that must be religiously followed. We suggest that schools use these characteristics as indicators of a healthy school culture and operationalize them by turning them into principles. Making these characteristics principles that can guide behavior creates the mindset that this is something to *do,* not simply a static list to evaluate a school or its staff.

Viewed dynamically, these characteristics become the means by which student performance can be improved. For example, we regard faculty collaboration as one sign of a good school culture (see also Lipsitz 1984, Rosenholtz 1985). At the same time, collaboration is also a vital mechanism for forging a common purpose, stimulating experimentation and innovation, and enhancing staff professionalism. If, when assessing a school's culture, it becomes obvious that there is no evidence of collective work toward mutually valued goals, then a project to establish collaborative relationships among the staff would be one target for an improvement project.

As another example, order and discipline are necessary ingredients of a school culture that encourages academic achievement (e.g., see MacKenzie 1983). If this element is missing, then strategies designed to establish it might be given priority in the early stages of an improvement project. One such strategy might be to use staff teams (or staff and student teams at the secondary level) to collaboratively devise ways to increase faculty control and student compliance. Here, collaboration is primarily a means to another end, yet the development of an increased capacity for and tendency to engage in collective problem solving is likely to result from this effort to institute better discipline.

Finally, these two examples highlight the interrelatedness of these 13 characteristics and the fact that they can serve, at different times in the change process, as means or ends or even both at once. Indeed, the strength of this approach to school improvement stems from its cultural grounding and from its merger of process and product.

## Guidelines for School Improvement

As the preceding discussion has indicated, the first step is to assess the school's culture using the 13 characteristics (or another research-based theme) as a guide. Our principle here is that change without solid information on the nature of the school as it now exists is likely to be mindless activism and an endlessly frustrating task. Following the dictum, "If it ain't broke, don't fix it," we urge that wholesale cultural change not be undertaken unless the situation clearly demands it. In most schools the cultural assessment will "red flag" a few areas of weakness where the change effort would be most profitably directed. While comprehensive change may ultimately be necessary to bring about the fundamental reform of schools (which is not the issue here), a selective change effort aimed at specific cultural targets is a more realistic endeavor for most schools.

Since our conception of culture stresses beliefs and practices ("the way we do things around here"), it follows that changing schools essentially means changing what the principal players in the learning process value and do regarding school. This is not easily accomplished, nor can it be done in the span of a few months.

Adopting a cultural perspective at the school level also means that attention must be paid to the peer culture of students, especially in secondary schools. Since student peer culture so strongly influences student performance, school staff members must be cognizant of whether the dominant peer culture adds to or detracts from the school's mission. In other words, how students see themselves in the context of the school, the extent to which they value academic success or willingly comply with school rules, will affect their achievement. Even though many of the determinants of peer culture lie outside the school's control (see Ogbu 1978, Willis 1977), schools can have an impact. So, in assessing the school's culture, staff members must also assess the dominant student culture and look for ways to mesh the two to make them mutually supportive of the school's mission.

Finally, symbols, rituals, and even myths play an important role in organizational cultures (Pettigrew 1979). Rituals or ceremonies contain messages about values and about the relative importance of a school's many, and often conflicting, goals. Moreover, rituals provide a "shared experience of belonging" (Pettigrew 1979, p. 576) and thereby contribute to identification with the school community. By expressing and reinforcing what the school values and by publicly acknowledging accomplishments, such ceremonies and symbols socially legitimize the school mission. As examples, academic pep assemblies, award banquets for families of students who have met personal improvement goals, and professional recognition and advancement for collaborating groups of teachers making extraordinary contributions to the school can be used to help manipulate the school's culture.

Returning to an earlier theme, the use of ceremonies is not a viable substitute for comprehensive change. Nevertheless, creating and using cultural symbols is not a difficult undertaking, and the efficacy of such symbols within an organization is probably best illustrated by the importance attached to them by many of the nation's most profitable corporations (e.g., see Peters and Waterman 1982).

## Concluding Thoughts on School Culture

We have digressed some distance into the area of school culture given that the focus of this book is on district organization. We think this excursion necessary. School culture and district culture are not one and the same. District culture sets the parameters within which school culture exists, and to some extent the two have a reciprocal (but largely unexplored) relationship. However, cultures differ across schools even within the same district. More importantly, school cultures are distinct from that of the district; the elements of a productive school culture are not necessarily identical with the components of a healthy district culture. Given the importance of culture to organizational effectiveness, it is essential that educators at all levels of the organization understand the nature and role of the school culture.

With this common understanding of the role and importance of school culture as a basis, we now turn to the topic of school leadership. While the discussion is focused on principal leadership, we will return to issues raised in this examination of school culture. In so doing, we will suggest a structural means to solidify the notion of school culture by the use of schoolwide problem-solving teams and decentralized decision making. We will also incorporate into the discussion themes (e.g., strategic planning, empowerment) that have been raised in previous chapters.

# PRINCIPAL LEADERSHIP

In the nonrational world that confronts educational organizations, the characteristics and behaviors desirable of leaders at the district level are equally appropriate for leaders at the school level. However, because there are obvious differences in the arenas in which central office and building leaders act, in their specific responsibilities, and in their relationship to resources and district policy decisions, it is helpful to look more closely at effective school leadership.

While it is not possible at this time to causally link principals' actions to the practices of teachers and the achievement of students (Manasse 1985), there is a growing conviction that certain behaviors by the principal are necessary, if not sufficient, to creating and maintaining good schools. We support this assumption, but we begin with five points that must be remembered when discussing the role of the principal.

## Five Cautions

1. While it seems to have become the common wisdom that principals are *the* key element, the principal is not, in fact, the only person who can provide leadership, especially leadership for school improvement (e.g., see Barth 1980, Gersten et al. 1982, Hall et al. 1983, Lieberman and Miller 1984, Purkey 1984). Not only is this a tremendous burden, given the demands of managing a school's daily affairs, but few principals have received the training that would equip them to be reform leaders, and the skills involved in administering the daily routine are likely to be different from the leadership skills required for innovation. To be sure, leadership is essential to the success of our schools, principals are advantageously positioned to provide it, and change is unlikely to happen in schools without principals' support. Nevertheless, leadership can come from teachers and other administrators. In this sense, good principal leadership may at times consist of finding, publicly recognizing, and supporting by word and deed the leadership of others in the school.

2. There is a tendency to describe the style of exemplary principals in stereotypic masculine terms leading to the presumption that all principals should resemble CEO's in industry, or be autocratic captains of an educational ship. Not only is there evidence that the style of effective principals may vary (e.g., Hargrove et al. 1981), but there is also evidence that leadership can assume another voice that, among other things, is more democratic and more sensitive to relations among people (Adkison 1981, Kanter 1975, Lightfoot 1983). The perceived need for a tough, masculine image places a straitjacket

on principals as they develop a personal style. More importantly, the masculine style is conducive to the myth of the rational organization (Borman and Spring 1984) in which strong leaders take unyielding stands, buttressed by certain knowledge in a one-best-way that is to be faithfully carried out by those beneath them. As we have argued, this is an inaccurate model of school organization, the more so because it does not square with the nature of principals' daily work.

3. Not only style but specific behaviors may vary among equally effective principals (e.g., see Duke and Imber 1983, Hansen 1979, Rutherford 1985). School context—which includes items such as the socioeconomic status of the school's population, the amount of community support or pressure, the history of reform efforts in the building, and the state of the relationship between teachers and administrators—is likely to strongly affect what a principal should (and can) do in any given situation. To think otherwise is to assume that schools are identical. While we argue that sound management principles are consistent across sites, it makes little sense to seek specific behaviors that must be universally and routinely applied.

4. What effective principals do in schools as they are presently constituted may be different from what they would do in institutions having an alternative organizational structure. For example, one image of an effective principal today is often of someone who bucks the system, who is a sort of maverick. We suggest this stems from the limits and inadequacies of the rational, bureaucratic model adopted by the central office, which can often result in principals having to go their own way in order to accomplish their schools' goals. If schools and districts were to acknowledge the reality of the nonrational model, and conduct themselves accordingly, it is likely that new behaviors or skills would be demanded of the effective principal. At the very least, we must be wary of developing lists of behaviors or skills derived only from what principals now do without paying attention to what good leaders do in organizations that more closely resemble the decentralized model we have been advocating.

5. The above comments about maverick principals notwithstanding, good leadership at the building level requires the support of the central office (Purkey and Smith 1985). Dumping the entire responsibility for educational excellence on the building principal on the grounds that he or she must become an instructional leader is not appropriate. Principals need assistance and training to learn leadership skills, they need support as they experiment with new forms of administering the school, and they need access to resources to enable them to implement their policies and programs. In discussing his management theory, Deming (1982), whom the Japanese credit as the

architect of their post-war industrial renaissance, asserts that in all cases of low quality (and productivity) the problem is in the system and only the top management can alter the system. Applied to educational organizations, this means that the superintendent and senior staff assume major responsibility for creating the conditions under which effective leadership can emerge at the building level.

## Effective Principals

With these five points in mind, the simplest thing that can be said about effective principals is that they act so as to bring about the characteristics of an effective school. That is, they attempt to establish a culture that encourages and facilitates teaching and learning. To accomplish this, a principal uses particular skills, engages in certain behaviors, and adopts specific attitudes all of which may vary according to the situation. Recently, various researchers have compiled rather convergent lists of these skills, behaviors, and attitudes (e.g., see Manasse 1985, Rosenholtz 1985, Rutherford 1985, Saphier and King 1985). These elements are then combined as principals carry out the tasks and assume the appropriate roles necessary to build a productive school culture. While different researchers emphasize different tasks and roles, there is general agreement that establishing a positive school culture involves skills related to the roles of manager, teacher, facilitator (i.e., human relations skills), politician, and analyst (e.g., Cunningham 1985, Sergiovanni 1984; see Cuban 1985 for a similar discussion of the roles of superintendent). These tasks and roles are found to be interrelated as well, which raises the point that principals may not need to be equally adept at every role or task since strength in one may well compensate for weakness in another. (Principals might concentrate on what they do well even as they seek assistance in improving their ability in other areas—they need not despair if they are not super-principal.)

# RELATIONSHIP BETWEEN EFFECTIVE SCHOOLS AND EFFECTIVE PRINCIPALS

To help clarify the relationship between effective schools and principal leadership, we turn to six areas in which the descriptions of each overlap.

First, both literatures recognize the importance of culture. For schools, a culture that supports teaching and learning is the mechanism that promotes high performance. School culture can also promote attachment to the school as an institution. Principals, therefore, should be able to assess the school's existing culture and understand the levers (symbols, ceremonies, rituals, etc.) by which inappropriate cultures can be transformed and productive cultures maintained.

Second, both literatures acknowledge the importance of local responsibility and control. In schools, a measure of autonomy is deemed necessary to "fit" the school to varying environmental, political, and historical conditions. At the same time, giving the staff responsibility for the school's organizational health leads to ownership and commitment and may be a prerequisite to releasing the innovative spirit within the school. Characteristically, effective principals assume responsibility for making their school "work." These principals seek and seize every opportunity to do what they think best for the school, sometimes even in the face of obstacles within the central office. Clearly, school site management is critical to a principal's ability to forge a responsive school culture.

Third, both literatures assert the importance of commonality of purpose. In schools, clear and shared goals provide unity, help channel and target resources within the school program, can foster collaboration, and establish criteria for school success that permit assessment of progress. Applied to principals, this takes the form of a clear vision of what the school should be, which is translated into concrete objectives and communicated to the staff in such a way as to influence what they do in their professional roles. For both the school and the principal, written school improvement plans can be a road map for creating and realizing a shared vision of what the school should be. (See Purkey 1984 for an example of the use of school improvement plans in a secondary school effectiveness project.)

Fourth, both literatures assume the importance of collaborative relationships and democratic decision making. Even though collaboration and shared decision making are not identical and one can exist without the other, both are essential to the successful implementation of educational change, both are thought to increase job satisfaction, and both are conducive to an environment of experimentation and mutual assistance. Effective principals, by example and by policy, support collaboration and involve staff in decision making. More concretely, they adopt the principle of empowerment (see Chapter 7) and establish participative teams, wherever possible, to solve problems and make decisions that affect the entire school.

Fifth, both the literature on effective schools and that on effective principals address the issue of stability. In schools, stability means that the staff stay together long enough to become familiar with each other, their students, and the school's structure and purpose. Achieving some characteristics of good schools (e.g., collaboration, community) requires extended time, and change by its very nature is a risky enterprise. Without knowing that they will be at the school for the long haul, staffs may find little incentive to take risks, even under pressure from the central office or the community; under such conditions, people play it safe and go by the book. Correspondingly, effective principals should take a long-term, patient view and seek to drive out fear of risk taking and innovation (and, we would add, are themselves not rotated from building to building as they move up the administrative ladder).

Sixth, both literatures emphasize the importance of maximized learning time. This takes a variety of forms in schools but certainly includes the maintenance of discipline and safety, the protection of the instructional program from interruption and interference, and the fullest use of the time available for learning. Principals need to ensure that these conditions are met and provide the resources teachers need to take advantage of their allotted classroom time. Effective principals also actively seek knowledge about curriculum and instruction that can be used to enhance their leadership as well as raise the level of staff members' teaching efficiency and effectiveness.

## Three Leadership Principles

Assuming that a school leader has become familiar with the literature on principal leadership and school effectiveness, and is aware of the high degree of congruence between them, what next? Unfortunately, there are no formulas that can be applied to the principalship. There are certain principles, however, that can offer guidance, even if they do not provide specific instructions in all cases.

One such principle, already mentioned, is to avoid the "if only" tendency of thinking that better teachers or a new instructional technology will solve a school's problems. The experience of the Chicago Public Schools with mastery learning (Olson 1985) should be warning enough that technologies, by themselves, cannot turn schools around. Also, unless there is evidence that the teachers are simply not trying to educate their students, it is unlikely that exhortations or goals posted as quotas (all our students will score above the 25th percentile!) will accomplish much. Instead, a more productive approach is to analyze the school's culture, determine what aspects of it (e.g., expectations, communication patterns, incentives) are obstacles to teaching and learning, and then intervene where necessary. Moreover, altering the structure and process of the school as an organization is likely to prove easier (but it is no easy task) than attempting to "fix" individual teachers or assemble a staff of master teachers (see O'Toole 1981).

The second principle is to think politically about how to get staff working together (Bacharach and Mitchell 1986). To think politically in this context means to analyze the school, not only culturally, but also in terms of its various constituencies and its key actors. (This is very similar to what we have called strategic planning at the district level.) One constituency in many secondary schools is the coaches, another is the "old guard" who have been in the school seemingly forever, and a third might be the "activists," the teachers who, as a group, are most receptive to innovation if they perceive it to be in their students' best interest. Other constituencies cluster around departments, academic versus vocational programs, and so on. At the elementary level the dynamics are usually less complicated, but here, too, interest groups can be identified, perhaps involving a division between upper and lower grade teachers or between newer (often younger) teachers and the school veterans.

To get staff to work together in such a situation, it is necessary to recognize the existence of these interest groups, to identify the influential staff within each group (keeping in mind that people often belong to more than one interest group), and to form teams that cut across these organizational segments (see Kanter 1983).

Improvement projects will often tread on the toes of one or another interest group. For example, altering course requirements to raise the number of academic classes a student must take will very likely encounter opposition from teachers whose classes are not counted as being academic. While a political strategy and team building approach will not do away with objections and conflict, it offers a way of successfully managing such disputes.

Applying these principles requires information about the school's culture and usable data on student performance. A general awareness of what is happening throughout the building and in its classrooms, which can be obtained only by walking around and talking with staff and students, is also necessary to the team building strategy. Note that recent commentators on educational quality have suggested that schools, for all the data they collect, are information poor when it comes to having useful indicators of cultural or systemic troublespots (e.g., see Goodlad 1984). At the same time, awareness is often listed as one of the characteristics of the effective principal (Manasse 1985).

Another aspect of what we call political thinking, and which contributes to building awareness, involves listening to the staff to find out what barriers exist that prevent them from teaching and from taking pride in what they do (Deming 1982). Principals must search for problems (and encourage their staff to do likewise). Though this may have a negative connotation for some, it is another dimension to the development of staff willingness to take risks (Giacquinta 1975) and is likely to contribute to the climate of experimentation and continuous change found in successful schools (Little 1982). Problems exist in all schools. Acknowledging that problems exist, responding to staff perceptions of problems, and jointly seeking solutions are all aspects of political behavior that build trust among the staff and serve as a necessary precondition of fundamental change.

To think politically also means to recognize that a vague vision without an accompanying constancy of specific purpose leads to frustration and cynicism (Deming 1982). Bombarded with fads and passing fancies, teachers (and administrators) find it all too easy to adopt a "this too shall pass" mentality. Since meaningful change does not magically appear overnight, constancy of purpose is essential to the long-term effort needed for school improvement. Moreover, constancy of purpose demonstrates to the staff that principals do what they say they are going to do when they said they would do it. This form of integrity helps to inspire trust on the part of the staff, which is necessary to risk taking and hence innovation.

The third principle is to empower others. The team building approach indicated by a political understanding of schools assumes, too, that decision-making power will be decentralized. Since the strategy of empowerment is treated in considerable depth in Chapter 7, we confine ourselves here to noting that delegating authority and democratizing decision making contribute to greater flexibility (via school site management) and greater responsibility for school reform at the school level (Purkey and Smith 1985). Simply put, people naturally have a greater investment in, and commitment to, those decisions that they participated in making. Whatever else empowerment accomplishes in terms of, for example, enhancing staff professionalism, it is a powerful mechanism for generating ownership by the people in whose hands success or failure inevitably rests.

Rarely will principals be able to single-handedly turn a school around. The principle of empowerment rests upon the postulate that getting staff to work in concert toward a common goal is likely to be much easier to the extent that they are meaningfully involved in the selection and implementation of school improvement projects. The dilemma of empowerment, and consequently a key leadership task, is to avoid the "too many cooks spoil the broth" phenomenon, thereby diluting reform to the point that serious change is not attempted. Empowerment, therefore, does not mean the abdication of authority or the relinquishment of leadership; leadership is essential to the implementation of significant innovations. Empowerment does mean, however, giving others the opportunity and responsibility to gain and wield influence.

## Concluding Thoughts

We close this discussion of principal leadership with two observations. First, although we draw heavily upon lessons from the private sector in describing principal leadership, schools, unlike most corporations, are public service organizations. In the end, the sole criterion by which the success of a corporation is judged is its profits. Schools, however, must meet equity criteria, and they have an obligation to be a healthy environment for the developmental growth of students (and staff). Without belaboring the point, in the attempt to achieve educational excellence there is always a danger of overlooking issues of equity and quality of institutional life. Efficiency and cost effectiveness are always paramount to a profitable corporation; they may not always be as critical to good schools. Along this vein, we agree with Manasse (1985) that it is an error to think of leadership skills and characteristics apart from how and to what ends they are applied. If the aims of education are inappropriate, then the best leadership will amount to little.

Second, teachers and other school administrators possess an ideology, have undergone training, and have accumulated a wealth of experiences. They tend to assume that they have an expertise that entitles them to a great deal of autonomy and discretion in meeting the needs of students. This sense of professionalism will mediate even the most forceful, dynamic leadership. And it should do so, albeit within limits, since the point is not to generate an employee mentality but to empower staff to take a more active, responsible role for the well-being of the whole school, as well as for each of their students. This professionalism partially accounts for the debate, negotiation, and compromise endemic to the nonrational model of school organization. Our view of school reality sees this as necessary and even healthy, but it complicates the task of providing effective leadership toward a unifying vision of what the school should be.

However, listening to the staff and gaining a picture of the school as they see it with all its perceived strengths and weaknesses can be instrumental in forging a common vision. While the principal is ideally situated to formulate and articulate, as well as shape, the school's goals, good leadership involves engaging the staff in forming that common vision.

In this section, we have suggested three principles that can guide the principal in acquiring and applying the skills and characteristics necessary to leadership in a nonrational organizational world. First, we urge that principals refrain from "if only" searches for quick-fix solutions in hopes of escaping the hard, time-consuming work necessary to creating a productive school culture. Second, we urge principals to think politically in the broadest sense of the term as they seek to understand and then change the school's culture. Third, we encourage principals to empower others and spread the responsibility for school success throughout the organization, thereby tapping the talents and energy of all.

# 10

# Restoring Efficacy to Schools in a Nonrational World

_____

_____

_____

_____

_____

## INTRODUCTION

We began this book by demonstrating that times are difficult for educators. Change, ambiguity, and crisis are the normal state of affairs. Educators have experienced a declining sense of efficacy as they attempted to apply old organizational models to this new state of affairs. Within the old model, despite the best intentions and vigorous efforts, educators experience less ability to make a positive difference in the lives of their students. Efforts seem frantic and results seem fragmentary: attention is divided in many contradictory directions. Things just don't seem to cohere any more. In the compelling image of the Irish poet William Butler Yeats, "Things fall apart; the center cannot hold" (Rosenthal 1962).

Throughout our discussion, we have said that, in order to restore this center and a sense of efficacy, educators must:

1. recognize the nature of the changes occurring in the world that forms the environment for elementary and secondary education;

2. recognize that there is a way of *thinking about and within* our educational organizations that may be more helpful than the traditional way; and

3. learn and use new strategies for setting goals, making decisions, planning, distributing power, structuring the organization, leading the organization, and thinking about teaching.

These ideas are based on a belief that organizations in general and educational organizations in particular are dependent on the context in which they are developed. We have characterized that context as one of rapid and massive social change. Such a context requires an organization that can adapt and adopt, if the organization is to be innovative, productive, and of high quality. We have contended that the integrated structures of the nonrational organization provide great promise for the effective education of multiple constituencies in a context of change.

We have argued that the nonrational model is a more powerful approach for dealing with our changing social reality than is the traditional rational model, partly because it pays systematic and continuous attention to current contexts. The rational model fails to include this activity, except in a periodic fashion. As an additional liability, the rational model leads to the creation of bureaucratic and segmented organizations. We have said such systems are ill-adapted for responding to present realities. In order to reestablish the context for these conclusions, let us briefly reiterate the nature of the changes facing education. This context creates the need for the nonrational model.

## SUMMARIZING CHANGE

### Changes in People

Thinking of schools as cultural phenomena (another way of saying contextually dependent), we began our discussion by demonstrating that significant social change is altering American society and our schools. Perhaps most notable are the demographic changes the society is experiencing. Students entering our schools are a vastly different group than they were even ten years ago. There are more minority students, more poor students, and more students from troubled backgrounds and nontraditional families. The social demography is further complicated by changes in immigration patterns and by changes in the age makeup of the population. The constituency that has a direct stake in education has diminished, as the number of families with children has declined to less than 30 percent.

These students represent a daily challenge to their teachers and principals, who have also changed. Educators as a group are older, and are going through life stages that may make it difficult for them to adjust to this new generation of students. One near-term consequence of this demographic situation will be a need for vast numbers of new educators to replace those who are retiring and defecting from the teaching and administrative ranks. Many of these people are leaving because of disillusionment and a reduced sense of efficacy in the context of the changed social reality. To define efficacy yet again, but in a slightly different way than previously, it is the power to make a positive difference, and we suggest that it comes from gaining coherent, consistent, effective, and positive results from one's professional actions.

## Changes in Expectations

Both legislative and local community expectations for schools have grown, and often these present conflicting demands. Resources to meet these demands are short; fiscal crisis is the norm, compounded by both the economic and social impact of collective bargaining on the culture of schools. The sense of frustration and ineffectiveness grows as educators try to respond to confusing expectations.

We said that one source contributing to both a sense of ineffectiveness and actual mediocre performance has been the clinging to outmoded assumptions about how organizations function. We presented alternatives to those assumptions.

## Changes in Thinking about Organizations

*The Rational Model—How Things Really Don't Seem to Work.* We argued that a disorienting, disintegrating, or incoherent state of affairs arises from imposing an outmoded model on our educational system in a world that has significantly changed. We called this model the *rational* model, and presented it straightforwardly in Chapter 2. Hallmarks of this model are:

- an orientation toward a single set of stable goals,
- a belief that power is a fixed entity flowing from the top down through a tightly coupled and segmented structure,
- logical decision making that carefully chooses the single best path among all available options informed by all relevant knowledge,
- operation in an environment that is stable and predictable, and
- a view of the teaching process that reduces that process to a single set of best practices.

It is important to reiterate that the rational model is how many people feel school systems *should* run and how the best ones *do* run. Our point has been that the former is not possible and the latter not true.

*The Nonrational Model—How Things Really Seem to Work.* It is clear that no explanatory framework can provide all the answers, but the *nonrational* framework provides the potential for more productive and higher quality work in a time of rapid change calling for adaptation and innovation. The nonrational model has its hallmarks too. First, we reiterate that nonrational does not mean irrational, and that schools do have a central mission— to improve learning and the quality of life in schools. Within that mission however:

• Goals can be multiple, competing, contradictory, ambiguous, and promoted by a variety of interest groups. Goals are chosen as much by their power to command attention as by their intrinsic importance.

• Decision making is closely tied to goal definition. Problems commanding the most attention get flagged for a decision. Final decisions are made from a limited range of options in a last-minute flurry of negotiations and compromise. Problems that ultimately are most important to the mission may be ignored if they can't command attention, either because they have no effective spokespersons or because they are too sensitive to be confronted directly.

• Power is an open-ended entity, available throughout the organization to those who have access to resources.

• The external environment is volatile and unpredictable; it intrudes at all points in the process.

• There is a range of situationally appropriate teaching methodologies.

• The connection between policymaking and classroom instruction is tenuous and loosely coupled.

Realizing the troubling nature of this view of the world, especially when contrasted with the appealing orderliness of the rational approach, we spent some time restating our belief that the nonrational view is a more accurate representation of reality; hence it is a more sensible approach to organizational life in a world filled with change and uncertainty. Perhaps the key to this part of the discussion is the reminder that schools now serve multiple constituencies. In the past, education's constituency was more uniform in its background and goals. Given multiple constituencies, our approach to goals, decision making, power, external environment, the teaching process, and centralized authority seems to make a better fit with that reality.

Amid the frequently shifting perspectives of the nonrational model, however, one of our most important points has been that nonrational decision makers need to be analytical, systematic, and logical. But these skills, exported from the rational model, take on new meaning in a nonrational world when they require augmentation by such strangers to the rational model as intuition, vision, and insight. These latter skills were pivotal in our discussion of nonrational leaders and how they integrate rational and nonrational skills into a unified complement of leadership behaviors.

Let us recall three areas of the nonrational model where leadership can be exercised.

# SUMMARIZING STRATEGIES OF THE NONRATIONAL MODEL

## The Importance of Culture

Given our belief that schools are cultural phenomena, it should not be surprising that understanding the culture of the organization is one of the most important activities in the nonrational approach to organizations. We defined two dimensions of culture—guiding beliefs and daily behavior—and provided tools for identifying these dimensions. We also provided an approach for using these dimensions to assess the health of the culture.

## Strategic Planning

For those who feel that the nonrational model represents an irresponsible approach to organizations, the chapter on strategic planning should have served as an antidote. Strategic planning does emphasize logic and analysis, but is a much more subtle and complex process than the artificial periodic and linear exercise of planning in the rational model. Our contrast of the production of master plans with masterful planning is more than just phrasemaking. A strategic plan is dynamic, and is constantly being monitored, interpreted, altered, improved, and, above all, implemented. The skills and knowledge needed to carry it out are more demanding than rational master planning. The emphasis on qualitative data, the need for both external and internal analysis, and the four dimensions of external data-gathering—economic, political, technological, and social—are enough in themselves to push most would-be educational planners into unfamiliar waters.

## Empowerment

In Chapter 7 we discussed empowerment—a key concept if organizations are to be able to respond effectively to our changing environment and the changing expectations of workers. We indicated that this was a key leadership behavior. By inference, effective leaders are willing and able to distribute power widely to people in the organizations; they do this by creating the integrated systems we have discussed previously, and by assuring that access to support, information, and resources flows throughout the organization.

## Leadership

Our discussion of leadership also emphasized the importance of the context. We purposely chose to avoid providing our version of the standard list of leadership skills and qualities. Instead, we stressed the importance of the effective leader adopting a more functional and holistic way of thinking about organizations—in short, the nonrational model. This approach required the would-be leader to understand and assess the world within and beyond organizations. Then the leader needed to develop a vision of the organization's future.

A variety of approaches was needed to develop this vision. Again, rather than providing a linear list of skills, we used four directional metaphors for vision: foresight, hindsight, depth perception, and peripheral vision. We suggested two important modes of thought in order to develop vision. Effective leaders needed a systematic method of scanning, monitoring, and interpreting events, in concert with a simultaneous past, present, and future orientation. In seeking images to describe this way of thinking, we used holistic concepts—the hologram, or the gestalt. An integrated synthesis of thought, with all faculties acting in concert, was what we were portraying.

## The Nonrational Model at the Building Level

Because of the concept's importance in the current knowledge base for effective schooling practices, building-level culture and leadership was explored at some length in Chapter 9. School cultures are not the same as district cultures; their importance in determining educational quality makes it imperative that educators who would be leaders understand how they function. We presented 13 characteristics that can be used to assess a school's culture. A major point was that effective principals create cultures that encourage and facilitate teaching and learning. Intriguing is the fact that the descriptions in the literature of effective schools overlap with descriptions of effective principals, an idea we will return to shortly.

After assessing the school culture, we presented three principles for altering culture: *reframing from "if only" thinking, thinking politically,* and *empowering others.* Principals who would be leaders will need to effectively use these principles. Empowering others is the same concept as put forward for district organizations in Chapter 7. Thinking politically is parallel to strategic planning, discussed in Chapter 6. "If only" thinking is probably one of the hidden hallmarks of the rational model, usually expressed in the form of "if only" we could get more control over the students, "if only" we could get more cooperation from the staff, or "if only" we could get more computers. This chapter discussed the important role that symbols, rituals, and even myths play in school cultures, just as in all organizational cultures. Effective leaders must have a clear understanding of culture's role in educational organizations. Only then can they effectively employ strategies to alter the culture and build effective structures.

## CONCLUSION: INTEGRITY AND EFFICACY

The chapter on leadership concluded with a discussion of integrity as the glue that holds the effective leader's actions together. We return to that centralizing concept once again in closing this book.

The roots of the words integrity and integration are the same, meaning to create unity out of diversity. To integrate organizationally, socially, mathematically, or any other way means to bring together disparate parts and make them into a coherent whole. This coherent whole is different; generally more than the logical sum of its parts.

Similarly, as a human trait, having integrity means to deal with the many challenges, problems, temptations, and possibilities of professional and personal life from a central point of view that integrates values, intention, and action so that, while the specific actions of the person of integrity may sometimes be hard to predict, the central value core, intent, and general effectiveness of those actions are always predictable. The person's actions are coherent.

A sense of efficacy arises when one knows that one's behavior is coherent—that intentions lead to the desired results and that the results are worthy. Trust and confidence arise in others when they believe they can count on coherence, competence, and integrity from superiors, colleagues, and subordinates.

Integrity is a concept that can also be associated with organizational behaviors, cultures, and beliefs. When the actions of the organization are integrated, they have integrity. And so, in the nonrational view of school systems, not only is the skilled leader with integrity at the center, but the system itself has this integrity, generated partly through its integrated systems. To say that an organization has integrity is to say that it is put together well, solid, and unshakable, with all components working in concert, and that it keeps its promises.

However, at the same time, the nonrational integrated organization remains open to the external environment and internally flexible—the adaptive and innovative organization we have been describing throughout this book.

When spoken of in this way, the organization begins to take on human characteristics. Just as out of the complex integrated systems that make up a human being comes a unified impression of that person, so, an integrated organization conceived in the nonrational model takes on character. As we mentioned above, it is intriguing that the descriptions of effective principals conceptually overlap the descriptions of effective schools.

It is perhaps in this final anthropomorphic image of the organization that we create the proper feeling of integrated wholeness for which we are reaching. The nonrational model, which uses the segmenting and analytical skills of the rational model as part of its method for achieving organizational understanding, goes beyond the rational model in developing the skills, often intuitive, that reach for integration and integrity. In this way, the nonrational model encompasses the rational, and becomes a significant further step in understanding and describing the complexity of human organizations. A new and more complex integration is achieved; greater integrity is given to our knowledge. The center will hold. From this central anchoring point comes a new ability to make results in school systems match our efforts and intentions. And just so, a sense of efficacy is restored.

# References

Adkison, J. A. "Women in School Administration: A Review of the Research." *Review of Educational Research* 51, 3 (Fall 1981): 317.

Agor, Weston H. "Tomorrow's Intuitive Leaders." *The Futurist,* August 1983, 49–53.

Anderson, C. S. "The Search for School Climate: A Review of the Research." *Review of Educational Research* 52, 3 (Fall 1982): 368–420.

Bacharach, Samuel B., ed. *Organizational Behavior in Schools and School Districts.* New York: Praeger Publishers, 1981.

Bacharach, Samuel B., Sharon C. Conley, and Joseph B. Shedd. *Education Reform and the American Teacher.* Ithaca, N.Y.: Organizational Analysis & Practice, Inc., 1986.

Bacharach, Samuel B., and Stephen M. Mitchell. "Schools as Political Systems." In *Handbook of Organizational Behavior,* edited by J. Lorsch. New York: Prentice-Hall, 1986.

Baldridge, J. Victor. "Strategic Planning in Higher Education: Does the Emperor Have Any Clothes?" In *The Dynamics of Organizational Change in Education,* edited by J. Victor Baldridge and Terrence E. Deal, 167–185. Berkeley: McCutchan Publishing Corporation, 1983.

Baldridge, J. Victor, and Terrence F. Deal, eds. *The Dynamics of Organizational Change in Education.* Berkeley: McCutchan Publishing Corporation, 1983.

Barth, R. *Run School Run.* Cambridge: Harvard University Press, 1980.

Bennis, Warren, and Burt Nanus. *Leaders.* New York: Harper & Row, 1985.

Berman, Paul, and Milbrey W. McLaughlin. *Federal Programs Supporting Educational Change, Volume VIII: Implementing and Sustaining Innovations,* R–1589/8-HEW. Santa Monica, Calif.: Rand Corporation, May 1978.

Blumberg, Arthur, and Phyllis Blumberg. *The School Superintendent.* New York: Teachers College Press, 1985.

Borman, K. M., and J. H. Spring. *Schools in Central Cities.* New York: Longman, 1984.

Boyer, E. L. *High School.* New York: Harper & Row, 1983.

Bradford, David L., and Allen R. Cohen. *Managing for Excellence.* New York: John Wiley & Sons, 1984.

Brookover, W. B., C. Beady, P. Flood, J. Schweitzer, and J. Wisenbaker. *School Social Systems and Student Achievement: Schools Can Make A Difference.* New York: Praeger, 1979.

Callahan, R.E. *Education and the Cult of Efficiency.* Chicago: University of Chicago Press, 1962.

Cohen, M. "Instructional, Management and Social Considerations in Effective Schools." In *School Finance and School Improvement: Linkages for the 1980s* (Fourth Annual Yearbook), edited by A. Odden and L. D. Webb. Cambridge: American Educational Finance Association, 1983.

Cohen, Michael D., and James G. March. *Leadership and Ambiguity.* New York: McGraw-Hill, 1974.

Coleman, J. S., T. Hoffer, and S. Kilgore. *High School Achievement: Public, Catholic and Private Schools Compared.* New York: Basic Books, 1982.

Cope, Robert G. *Strategic Planning, Management, and Decision Making.* Washington, D.C.: American Association for Higher Education, 1981.

Corwin, Ronald G. *A Sociology of Education.* New York: Appleton-Century-Crofts, 1965.

Cuban, L. "Conflict and Leadership in the Superintendency." *Phi Delta Kappan* 67, 1 (September 1985): 28–30.

Cunningham, Luverne L. "Leaders and Leadership: 1985 and Beyond." *Phi Delta Kappan* 67, 1 (September 1985): 17–20.

Darling-Hammond, Linda. *Beyond the Commission Reports: The Coming Crisis in Teaching.* Santa Monica, Calif.: The Rand Corporation, July 1984.

Davis, Stanley M. *Managing Corporate Culture.* Cambridge: Ballinger Publishing Company, 1984.

Deal, Terrence E., and Allan A. Kennedy. *Corporate Cultures.* Reading, Mass.: Addison-Wesley Publishing Company, 1982.

Deal, Terrence E., and Allan A. Kennedy. "Culture and School Performance." *Educational Leadership* 40, 5 (1983): 14–15.

Deming, W. Edwards. *Quality, Productivity, and Competitive Position.* Cambridge: Massachusetts Institute of Technology, Center for Advanced Engineering Study, 1982.

Duke, D. L., and M. Imber. "Should Principals Be Required to Be Effective?" Unpublished paper, Lewis and Clark College, Portland, Oregon, 1983.

Eberts, Randall W., and Joe A. Stone. *Unions and Public Schools: The Effect of Collective Bargaining on American Education.* Lexington, Mass: D.C. Heath and Company, 1984.

Edmonds, R. R. "Effective Schools for the Urban Poor." *Educational Leadership* 37, 1 (October 1979): 15–27.

Feistritzer, C. Emily. *Cheating Our Children: Why We Need School Reform.* Washington, D.C.: National Center for Educational Information, 1985a.

Feistritzer, C. Emily. *The Condition of Teaching: A State-by-State Analysis, 1985.* Lawrenceville, N.J.: Princeton University Press, 1985b.

Fullan, Michael, and Alan Pomfret. "Research on Curriculum and Instruction Implementation." *Review of Educational Research* (Winter 1977): 391–392.

Gallup, Alec M. "The 17th Annual Gallup Poll of the Public's Attitudes Toward the Public Schools." *Phi Delta Kappan* 67, 1 (September 1985): 35–47.

Gersten, R., D. Carnine, and S. Green. "The Principal as Instructional Leader: A Second Look." *Educational Leadership* 40 (December 1982): 47–50.

Giacquinta, J. B. "Status Risk-Taking: A Central Issue in the Initiation and Implementation of Public School Innovations." *Journal of Research and Development in Education* 9, 1 (1975): 102–114.

Goodlad, J. I. *A Place Called School.* New York: McGraw-Hill, 1984.

Greenhalgh, John. *School Site Budgeting.* Lanham, Md.: University Press of America, Inc., 1984.

Guzzetti, B. *Report on Instruments for Measuring School Effectiveness.* Denver: Mid-Continent Regional Education Laboratory, 1983.

Hall, G. E., S. M. Hord, L. L. Huling, W. L. Rutherford, and S. M. Stiegelbauer. *Leadership Variables Associated with Successful School Improvement.* Research and Development Center for Teacher Education, University of Texas at Austin, Report No. 3164, April 1983.

Hansen, E. *Educational Administration and Organizational Behavior.* Boston: Allyn and Bacon, 1979.

Hargrove, E. C., S. G. Graham, L. E. Ward, V. Abernethy, J. Cunningham, and W. K. Vaughn. *Regulations and Schools: The Implementation of Equal Education for Handicapped Children.* Nashville: Vanderbilt University, Institute for Public Policy Studies, 1981.

Hawley, W. D., S. J. Rosenholtz, with H. Goodstein and T. Hasselbring. "Good Schools: What Research Says About Improving Student Achievement." *Peabody Journal of Education* 61, 4 (Summer 1984).

Hickman, Craig R., and Michael A. Silva. *Creating Excellence: Managing Corporate Culture, Strategy, and Change in the New Age.* New York: New American Library, 1984.

Hodgkinson, Harold L. *All One System: Demographics of Education, Kindergarten Through Graduate School.* Washington, D.C.: Institute for Educational Leadership, Inc., 1985.

Johnson, Susan Moore. *Teacher Unions in Schools.* Philadelphia: Temple University Press, 1984.

Kanter, Rosabeth Moss. "Women and the Structure of the Organization: Explorations in Theory and Behavior." In *Another Voice,* edited by Marcia Millman and Rosabeth M. Kanter. Garden City: Anchor, 1975.

Kanter, Rosabeth Moss. *Men and Women of the Corporation.* New York: Basic Books, 1977, chapter 7.

Kanter, Rosabeth Moss. *The Change Masters.* New York: Simon and Schuster, 1983.

Kilmann, Ralph H. *Beyond The Quick Fix: Managing Five Tracks to Organizational Success.* San Francisco: Jossey-Bass, 1984.

Kilmann, Ralph H. "Managing All Barriers to Organizational Success." *Training and Development Journal* (September 1985): 64–72.

Kirst, Michael W. "The Changing Balance in State and Local Power to Control Education." *Phi Delta Kappan* 66, 3 (November 1984): 189–191.

Leithwood, K. A., and D. J. Montgomery. "The Role of the Elementary School Principal in Program Improvement." *Review of Educational Research* 52, 3 (Fall 1982): 309–339.

Lewis, James, Jr. *Long Range and Short Range Planning for Educational Administrators.* Newton, Mass.: Allyn and Bacon, Inc., 1983.

Lewis, James, Jr. *Achieving Excellence in Our Schools...By Taking Lessons from America's Best-Run Companies.* Westbury, N.Y.: Institute for Advancing Educational Management, 1986.

Lezotte, L. W., and B. A. Bancroft. "Growing Use of the Effective Schools Model for School Improvement." *Educational Leadership* 42, 6 (March 1985): 23–27.

Lieberman, Ann, and Lynne Miller. *Teachers, Their World, and Their Work.* Alexandria, Va.: Association for Supervision and Curriculum Development, 1984.
Lightfoot, S. L. *The Good High School.* New York: Basic Books, 1983.
Lipsitz, J. *Successful Schools for Young Adolescents.* New Brunswick, N.J.: Transaction, 1984.
Little, J. W. "Norms of Collegiality and Experimentation: Workplace Conditions of School Success." *American Educational Research Journal* 19, 3 (1982): 325–340.
Lortie, Dan C. *School Teacher: A Sociological Study.* Chicago: University of Chicago Press, 1975.
Maccoby, Michael. *The Gamesman.* New York: Simon and Schuster, 1976.
MacKenzie, D. E. "Research for School Improvement: An Appraisal of Some Recent Trends." *Educational Researcher* 12, 4 (1983): 5–17.
Manasse, A. Lorri. "Improving Conditions for Principal Effectiveness: Policy Implications of Research." *The Elementary School Journal* 85, 3 (January 1985): 439–463.
March, James, and Johan P. Olsen. *Ambiguity and Choice in Organizations.* Oslo, Norway: Universitetsforlaget, 1976.
McCormack-Larkin, M. "Ingredients of a Successful School Effectiveness Project." *Educational Leadership* 42, 6 (March 1985): 31–37.
Miller, Lawrence M. *American Spirit.* New York: William Morrow and Company, Inc., 1984.
Miller, S. K., S. R. Cohen, and K. A. Sayre. "Significant Achievement Gains Using the Effective Schools Model." *Educational Leadership* 42, 6 (March 1985): 38–43.
Ogbu, J. U. *Minority Education and Caste: The American System in Cross-Cultural Perspective.* New York: Academic Press, 1978.
Olson, L. "Board of Education Stops Mastery Reading Program." *Education Week* 9, 41 (August 21, 1985): 1.
O'Toole, J. *Making America Work.* New York: Continuum, 1981.
Peters, T. J., and R. H. Waterman. *In Search of Excellence.* New York: Harper & Row, 1982.
Pettigrew, A. M. "On Studying Organizational Cultures." *Administrative Science Quarterly* 24 (December 1979): 570–581.
Protheroe, Nancy, Annette Lowell, and Susan Phillips. *Educator Opinion Poll Teachers: Opinions and Status?* Arlington, Va.: Educational Research Service, 1985.
Purkey, S. C. "School Improvement: An Analysis of an Urban School District Effective Schools Project." Doctoral diss., University of Wisconsin-Madison, 1984. (*Dissertation Abstracts International,* 45, 1926A; University Microfilms No. 85–15, p. 575.)
Purkey, S. C., and M. S. Smith. "Effective Schools: A Review." *The Elementary School Journal* 83, 4 (1983): 427–452.
Purkey, S. C., and M. S. Smith. "School Reform: The District Policy Implications of the Effective Schools Literature." *The Elementary School Journal* 85, 3 (January 1985): 353–389.
Raywid, Mary Anne, Charles A. Tesconi, Jr., and Donald R. Warren. *Pride and Promise.* Westbury, N.Y.: American Educational Studies Association, 1984.
Rhodes, Lewis. "Memo to the High School Futures Network." Correspondence, February 21, 1986.
Rosenholtz, S. J. "Effective Schools: Interpreting the Evidence." *American Journal of Education* 93, 3 (May 1985): 352–388.

Rosenthal, M. L., ed. "The Second Coming," William Butler Yeats, 1920. In *Selected Poems and Two Plays of William Butler Yeats*. New York: Macmillan Company, 1962, p. 91.

Rubin, Irene. "Retrenchment, Loose Structure, and Adaptability in the University." In *The Dynamics of Organizational Change in Education,* edited by J. Victor Baldridge and Terrence E. Deal. Berkeley: McCutchan Publishing Corporation, 1983.

Rutherford, W. L. "School Principals as Effective Leaders." *Phi Delta Kappan* 67, 1 (September 1985) 31–34.

Rutter, M., B. Maughan, P. Mortimore, J. Ouston, and A. Smith. *Fifteen Thousand Hours: Secondary Schools and their Effects on Children.* Cambridge: Harvard University Press, 1979.

Saphier, J., and M. King. "Good Seeds Grow in Strong Cultures." *Educational Leadership* 42, 6 (March 1985): 67–74.

Sarason, S. B. *The Culture of the School and the Problem of Change.* Boston: Allyn & Bacon, 1971.

Scott, W. R. *Organizations: Rational, Natural and Open Systems.* Englewood Cliffs, N.J.: Prentice-Hall, 1981, chapter 2.

Sergiovanni, T. J. "Leadership and Excellence in Schooling." *Educational Leadership* 41, 5 (February 1984): 4–13.

Sizer, T. R. *Horace's Compromise: The Dilemma of the American High School.* Boston: Houghton Mifflin, 1984.

Teddlie, C., C. Falkowski, S. Stringfield, S. Desselle, and R. Garvue. *The Louisiana School Effectiveness Study: Phase Two, 1982–84.* Baton Rouge: Louisiana State Department of Education, 1984.

Weick, K. "Educational Organizations as Loosely Coupled Systems." *Administrative Science Quarterly* 21 (1976): 1–19.

White A. N. *The Aims of Education.* New York: Macmillan, 1929.

Willis, P. E. *Learning to Labour.* Lexington, Mass.: D. C. Heath and Company, 1977.

Wise, Arthur. "Why Educational Policies Often Fail: The Hyperrationalization Hypothesis." Chapter 5 in *The Dynamics of Organizational Change in Education,* edited by J. Victor Baldridge and Terrence E. Deal. Berkeley: McCutchan Publishing Corporation, 1983.

# About the Authors

**Jerry L. Patterson,** Ph.D., is assistant superintendent for instruction of the Madison, Wisconsin, Metropolitan School District. He was appointed to this position in July 1983. Patterson has served in Kentucky, Ohio, Virginia, and Wisconsin in the various roles of high school teacher, curriculum consultant, research and evaluation specialist, university lecturer, and elementary principal. He has published extensively in the field of curriculum and instruction, with over two dozen articles in professional journals to his credit. In addition, Patterson recently authored a nationally recognized book on using computers in schools, published by Prentice-Hall, Inc. He has been selected as keynote speaker for conferences and workshops at the state, regional, and national level. He also serves as consultant to school districts and other educational agencies.

**Stewart C. Purkey,** Ph.D., is an assistant professor of education at Lawrence University in Appleton, Wisconsin, and is a researcher with the National Center on Effective Secondary Schools, University of Wisconsin–Madison. He has published articles on school effectiveness and educational policy. In addition to those two areas, his research interests are secondary education and organizational theory.

**Jackson VanBuren Parker III,** Ph.D., is administrative assistant for planning, information, and research in the Racine, Wisconsin, School District. He is a former teacher, university lecturer, and principal of a nationally acclaimed alternative secondary school, Walden III. He has led strategic planning teams, and is a frequent presenter at state and regional conferences. Parker has published extensively, most recently in the areas of demography, change in family structure, and school system organizational theory.